The Most Selfish Woman in America

How To Make Your Divorce
the Best Thing That Ever
Happened To You!

CHRISTIA SALE

Balboa Press books may be ordered through booksellers or by contacting:

Balboa Press
A Division of Hay House
1663 Liberty Drive
Bloomington, IN 47403
www.balboapress.com
1-(877) 407-4847

Because of the dynamic nature of the Internet, any Web addresses or links contained in this book may have changed since publication and may no longer be valid. The views expressed in this work are solely those of the author and do not necessarily reflect the views of the publisher, and the publisher hereby disclaims any responsibility for them.

The author of this book does not dispense medical advice or prescribe the use of any technique as a form of treatment for physical, emotional, or medical problems without the advice of a physician, either directly or indirectly. The intent of the author is only to offer information of a general nature to help you in your quest for emotional and spiritual well-being. In the event you use any of the information in this book for yourself, which is your constitutional right, the author and the publisher assume no responsibility for your actions.

Any people depicted in stock imagery provided by Thinkstock are models, and such images are being used for illustrative purposes only.

ISBN: 978-1-4525-3213-4 (sc)
ISBN: 978-1-4525-3215-8 (dj)
ISBN: 978-1-4525-3214-1 (e)

Library of Congress Control Number: 2011900478

Printed in the United States of America

Balboa Press rev. date: 2/16/2011

For Christen and Ryan

for whom my love will transcend space and time

Contents

Introduction

The Beginning of Your New Life

Welcome to your ***NEW LIFE!*** It is time for you to become ***A SELFISH WOMAN!***

Think about it this way: **YOUR DIVORCE MAY BE THE BEST THING THAT EVER HAPPENED TO YOU!** Really!

You may not feel that way now, but by the end of this book, you will be a new person. You will see the light! You will see your potential. Feel new zest for life. Be excited to finally be the person you've always dreamed of being. Live the life you've always dreamed of living.

There are two types of women in this situation. The women who tried to hold on to their marriage, for whatever reason . . . kids, love, etc. Then there are the women who caused the divorce in the first place. This book is for the former. The latter can give this book to a friend in need.

Repeat after me:
"I will do **what** I want, **when** I want, because **I Deserve It!"**

I'll wait here for you to say that a few more times . . . .

This is your new mantra.

If you are like me, you are newly divorced, with children either leaving the nest, or about to. You have just been through Hell and back. Your eyes are still slinging back and forth in your head like those cartoon characters!

Well, sit down, take a deep breath, and continue reading.

I will bring you back to the land of the living. I will show you how to stop the madness, reassess your goals, and redirect your life.

I am *demanding* that you start thinking of yourself *first* from this point forward!

I am *giving* you permission to be the Leading Lady in your own life!

I am *giving* you permission to be **SELFISH!**

S--selfish--putting yourself first because **It's Your Turn, Damn it!**
E--energetic lifestyle--tapping into what makes you vibrant, vivacious, and dynamic
L--laughter--enjoying life and choosing a positive attitude
F--feeding your body with clean, lean, natural foods
I--intelligence--feeding your mind and soul through traveling, exploring, learning and loving
S--success--being your successful, powerful woman you were meant to be
H--being *Happy* with the *New You*, and the *New Life* you've created!

In this book I will teach you:

- how to release the old life and create a new, happier one
- how not to get paralyzed by the chaos of change
- how to give yourself permission to put *Yourself first*
- how not to listen to those old, negative tapes, but make new, positive ones
- how to refuse to participate in vengeance
- how to stay focused on the *New You*

I will not:

- condone revenge
- throw you a pity party
- let you get calloused from your experience.

Your Old Life

The fact that your marriage has ended in divorce means that it was already a bad scene. And good riddance! For whatever reason--unfaithfulness, unstable personality, abusive treatment--*it's over*. And you survived. It was time to stop the madness! You're free!

You are battered and bruised, whether emotionally or physically, or both. You are completely spent. Sucked dry. Drained of your zest for life.

Exhausted from the constant stress and uneasiness of HIS coming home from work, or just walking into the room. Tiptoeing on egg shells all the time is painful. Your feet bleed, just like your heart. Your newly acquired irritable bowel syndrome is a constant reminder of how bad things have gotten. You grind your teeth so badly at night that you are lucky you still have any. Not to mention never having more than a shallow night's sleep . . . just in case.

Doubt and insecurity have crept into your subconscious, telling you that you aren't good enough to make it work. You're just not sexy enough, or pretty enough, or cook well enough, or make a home inviting enough for him to cherish--whatever. That low burn in your chest that sometimes makes you go into the bathroom, lock the door, and cry, where no one can see your pain . . . .

Well, enough of that! That was your **Old Life**. This is the beginning of your **New Life**.

Like I said, your divorce may be the best thing that ever happened to YOU!

You don't deserve to live that way! No one does. Don't let that old life define you anymore. And don't beat yourself up over it. Be glad you are free!

You could never have made the marriage work by yourself anyway. You can never truly change someone. Once you realize this fact, there is hope for your freedom. The most important thing is for you to release yourself from the emotional obligation and forgive yourself for the outcome. Remember, it takes two.

It's better to be alone and happy than to be with someone who makes you feel inferior, undesirable, not good enough, not smart enough . . . *stop me!*

So, it's time to shed this old skin and let the glow of your new skin shine.

Women are strong, always have been. Time has not changed that. Sometimes we just forget. We get lost in the everyday events and don't realize that we are spiraling down into a hole. Yet, once that reality sinks in, we can't see how to get out.

We get lost in our roles as mother, wife, daughter, PTA chair, Sunday school teacher, business tycoon, secretary, whatever. We wake up one day and wonder how we ever got here . . . and why aren't we happy? And who is *that* lying next to me?

Then one day our world that we thought we had control of falls apart. For whatever reason, it happens. I don't remember being consulted!

Wait a minute . . . I wasn't ready!

Such is life. So, now you have to regroup and get back to your core. Your *real, basic, true* self.

You won't be the same woman you were before. But that's a good thing. You will be stronger, smarter, and wiser. You will never let this happen again. You will start making better choices . . . **This is Good!**

Your New Life

This is what I'm here for. To help you come toward the light. To help you see that you were meant for greater things.

You have a whole other half of your life to live. You have plenty of time to find the "real you" and let her blossom. To enjoy life the way you always wanted to, explore the world, learn new things, and maybe even find your true soul mate in the process.

Considering the way things have turned out, you are *lucky* to have another chance. Now you know what you want and what you *don't* want. You will make better choices this time. You are wiser, stronger, and more confident in your decisions. Less tolerant of "users." More appreciative of what's really important in life.

Life will get so much clearer and easier when you take control of your outcome. You will gain self-respect and the respect of others when you dictate your future. No one else can derail you now. Don't let them! You have to get your goals into focus and laser in on them.

Also, refuse to get sucked up in the chaos of vengeance. Choose to take the high road. Whether kids are involved or not, this is the only answer. Don't participate in the mudslinging, name-calling, and accusations. This will just keep you entrenched in that negative life you are trying to get out of. Your old life will have a power over you as long as you choose to participate. The longer you breathe energy into that old story, the longer it will control you. And again, we need to lead and teach by example. As Kat Edmonson says in one of her songs, "*Be* the change that you want to *see*."

It may be hard at first to not defend your side of the story. Believe me, I've been there, Sister! But it is a relentless task that will never be achieved. For some reason, people love to get involved in other people's drama. You can't stop them. But you can refuse to be a part of perpetuating the negative. Otherwise, you just subject yourself to more of the same. And we aren't participating, right?

Your *Dream Life*

Now it is time for you to reassess your life. You have been given this new opportunity to accomplish the life you have always dreamed of. What ever that vision is, don't let this chance go to waste!

Your new goal is achieving your ***Dream Life***--the life you were meant to live. Whatever form it takes, *that* is your new focus.

Your ***Dream Life*** is the image you've always had of your "ultimate existence." That vision of you leading the masses, curing cancer, having your own clothing line, or being President . . . work with me here. And only you know what that image looks like. So, your first assignment is to think about what your ***Dream Life*** looks like, how it feels, what you are doing, what you are wearing, what you are driving, where you are living. Picture the whole package. Don't edit the vision. Now imagine YOU living that life . . . smile on your face and all.

Start thinking as if it is real. The more detail you can give this image, the more powerful it becomes. You **are** this person, you **are** living this life. Like T. Harv Eker says in *Secrets of the Millionaire Mind, Mastering the Inner Game of Wealth*, "What you focus on expands." So will your ***Dream Life***.

Change the way you see yourself, the decisions you make, the way you project yourself to reflect this new vision. See it in your mind, live it in your daily life, be it in your soul. Live life as if your dream is your reality. Base almost every decision on whether it brings you closer to your ***Dream Life***.

Here is the question I want you to ask yourself when you are not sure how to respond to *life*: **"Does this get me any closer to living my *Dream Life*?"**

If the answer is yes, do it and do it well. If the answer is no, then don't do it. Period. Next!

Embrace this new way of thinking and seeing yourself. Have the discipline to stop participating in the chaos. Stop listening to those old tapes. No more perpetuating the negative. You will never accomplish the lessons in this book if you don't make the break, NOW!

Clean break, new slate, fresh start. Now how's that for liberating?

Your NEW LIFE Declarations:

"I will do what I want, when I want, because **I Deserve It!**
"I am going to live my ***Dream Life***."
"I am going to make the most of my fresh start!"

"IT'S MY TURN!"

Your NEW LIFE Action Steps:

1. **Forgive yourself!**
2. Give yourself permission to be **SELFISH!**
3. Do what you want, when you want. Period. Don't just say it--do it!
4. Be the Leading Lady in your own life!
5. Let go of your "old life" and laser focus in on your "New Life."
6. Do NOT listen to those old tapes *ever again!*
7. Refuse to participate in the negative.
8. Every morning when you wake up, before you get out of bed, visualize your ***Dream Life***.
9. Every night before you go to sleep, visualize your ***Dream Life***, down to the last detail.
10. Be thankful that you have been given a new chance.
11. Thank God for your New Life!

Step One

S Is for SELFISH

I am giving **YOU** permission to be **SELFISH**! It is **YOUR** turn, damn it!

It is **YOUR** turn to be the **Leading Lady** in **YOUR LIFE**!

It's time to compartmentalize your *old life*, take the lessons from it, and go on to your *new life*. The sooner you release your old negative life, the sooner you will release the power it has over you. Some people let their ego and pride get in the way and follow that little green monster over to the dark side. Vengeance sucks the life out of you. We have no use for that here. It is time to accomplish your ***Dream Life***--the life you were meant to live!

Your EX, your old life, all those old tapes only have the power over you that you give them. You can completely disarm them by taking that power away. It is all in how you choose to respond. It's all in your control.

No Fear for the Free!

You realize that you are free now, right? Free to *be* and *do* whatever you have always dreamed of *being* and *doing*. The real YOU that somehow got lost in the struggle is waiting to come to life.

It's time to stop living in fear. The fear of not meeting the expectations of others. The fear of doing something new and out of your comfort zone. The fear of shaking up your world.

Well, Sister, your world is already shaken up. The fault is unimportant. The results are. "Fear of the EX" is not your ruler anymore!

This year it's all about YOU. The rest of your *LIFE* is all about YOU. It's about your pleasure, your happiness, and your success. It's about doing what YOU want to do, not what other people think you should do.

You've had enough of that. You've been doing that your whole life. What your parents thought you should do, your boss thought you should do, your children thought you should do, your husband thought you should do . . . enough already! You've also spent most of your life serving other people and being the last one served. Your career, your children, your husband, your church, your community . . . again, no wonder you are exhausted!

You may not be *comfortable* thinking of yourself first, which is understandable. It goes against everything you were taught as a girl growing up in America. But all those lessons you learned then don't apply to your life now. Putting everyone else's needs before your own, being meek and humble, being submissive . . . those aren't relevant any more.

That was your *old life*. This is your *new life*. Now it is time for you to put yourself first and do what YOU have a passion for. YOU were lucky enough to be given a new start. Use it!

Now let's recap. Something happened to cause your divorce. Whatever the reason, the fact is that it happened. And now it's time for you to take control of your situation. No one else is going to do it for you. Yes, you may not have wanted the divorce, but the reality is that it happened. You have to be disciplined and GET OVER IT! Wallowing in self-pity is not going to change the outcome. As long as you have a pity party for yourself, the past will have power over you. And we don't want that. Also, remember, if *the EX* did "it" once, *he* would do it again, and that applies to a myriad of things. Most people don't get over a lack of good judgment or integrity. And you can never change someone from who they truly are anyway.

Don't continue to subject yourself to that chaos. It's time to *shed* the old and *demand* the new. Dwelling on the facts will not change the outcome. You can only learn what you *don't* want again, and what you *do* want for your future.

You don't want to continue living with what caused your divorce in the first place. Things don't ever go back to the way they once were. Once change is initiated, things are never the same again. The fact that this even happened means he wasn't looking out for your best interest anymore. And that's not acceptable. YOU deserve better, and now YOU can demand it. Don't let anyone else define you like that again. YOU take control and define yourself.

Now that you have the freedom to choose, *what* is it that YOU really want to be? *Who* is it that YOU really want to be? Your answer to these questions will change everything!

I'm not here to lull you into a state of "I'll think about changing." I'm here to snap you out of that!

You've shed about 200 pounds recently, am I right? In the form of a man? A weight has literally been lifted. I call that "a new start." In my life, it was a miracle!

Now YOU are the master of your own destiny. If YOU want to reinvent yourself, do it! YOU have the freedom to change. A new life, free from the burden of the "wrong" man.

YOU have to start thinking of yourself in a new way. YOU are beautiful, smart, courageous, powerful, and in control. YOU may not feel that way now, but you will by the end of this book. For now, "act as if" you are.

Act as if you are as beautiful on the outside as you are on the inside. *Act as if* you are a smart, courageous woman who is wiser and braver. *Act as if* you are a powerful force who will be in control of her future. *Act as if* you are the person you've always wanted to be. *Act it* and *believe it!*

You will subconsciously bring these thoughts into existence. This is the Law of Attraction. As described in the book The Law of Attraction: The Basics of the Teachings of Abraham, you attract what you think about, whether you want it or not. And like T. Harv Eker says in his book *Secrets of the Millionaire Mind*, that which you focus on expands. Whatever you dwell on comes to be. So, instead of dwelling on how horrible things used to be and perpetuating more of the same, focus on your positive new life, how it makes you feel. Focus on *that* being your reality. Now, wouldn't you rather have that vision come true? I thought so.

Remember, if YOU believe it, they believe it. If YOU act confident, courageous, and powerful, you will believe it, and so will other people. If you act in control of your life, you will be. This is the power of the mind!

You can change how you are perceived in your own mind and in the minds of others. If you appear weak and sad, that is how you will see yourself and that is how others will see you. You will be perpetuating your *old life* again. But if you appear strong and in control, that is how you will be viewed. You will be reinforcing your *new life*.

Now, normally I don't promote even caring about what other people think. What's important is what YOU think. But the fact is that, to some extent, it does matter when it comes to your image. As long as other people are an active component in our lives, their perception of us matters. If you are projecting a strong, confident image, others are more likely to contribute positively to your efforts. And if your ***Dream Life*** depends on the interaction of others for it's business success, well you see what I mean.

YOU set the stage for your recovery. You will accelerate your healing by projecting the image you want to become. It is all in your control. Be convincing!

Now Back to Making Your *Dream Life* Your Reality

Our goal here is to make this new ***Dream Life*** happen. YOU need to feel the power and fire that you already have within you. It's there, it just needs to be stoked to a roaring blaze. You have been smoldering all along. That fire has just been suppressed and needs to be brought back to life. But it's there . . . burning.

The key to success is to *see* what you want, *live* what you want, and *be* what you want to be. It is powerful!

See it!
Live it!
Be it!

The Law of Attraction will fall into place and contribute to making your ***Dream Life*** your reality. But you have to do your part, which is . . . repeat after me:

See it!
Live it!
Be it!

Never underestimate the power of visualization. If you can visualize your ***Dream Life***, you can accomplish it. If you can get to the point that you can see every detail, you can make your dream your reality. Where you will live, what you will wear, what car you will drive, how big your bank account will be, what your net worth will be, the smile on your face . . . if you can see it in your mind, you can make it happen.

Also, the more detail you give your vision, the *sooner* it will become a reality. And don't edit yourself. Be as lavish in your vision as you want to be in your life. You are only as limited as your imagination and belief in yourself!

Start the new career that you always dreamed of. Move to your favorite foreign country or to a Caribbean island. Now is the time to stretch yourself. It's time to live that dream you've had in the back of your mind when you were changing those diapers, working for that almighty paycheck, or "laughing" at *the EX's* stupid jokes.

About the diaper reference, don't get me wrong. No one loves their kids more than I do. I am truly blessed to have them in my life. But they are getting older and will soon move on with their lives. And it's my *and your* turn to do the same. Just do it! Write that book, start designing clothes, take those dance classes, become a stand-up comedian, start singing, become a teacher. Whatever it is, there is no better time than the present to make that happen. You are already starting fresh in other aspects of your life (in between men, shall we say?). Why not your career, too?

You may already be in your dream job, and more power to you. If so, get back to climbing that corporate ladder, teaching the next leaders of the free world, or bringing consciousness to people in need. Whatever your goals are, focus on making them happen.

Get Comfortable with Attention

It is really important for you to get outside your comfort zone right now. You need to become comfortable with attention. People who are confident, vibrant, and happy attract attention. And that is going to be YOU!

Go to a wine bar or sit on the patio of your favorite restaurant by yourself. Yes, I said by yourself. Dress for attention (tastefully, of course) and practice handling the gazes. It's good for you to get used to dealing with attention of all types. Be it from men or women, get used to eyes being on you. Whether it is from attraction or envy, you need to be at ease with the spotlight. Because like I said, vibrant, happy people attract attention and you want to be comfortable with that.

Remember, everybody has their own baggage that they bring to the party. And it taints the way they see others. But what's important is that you learn to deal with the bad and appreciate the good. And in the meantime, you develop a strong sense of self.

Let them look. It's refreshing to see a confident woman with style and expression gracing a beautiful outdoor patio, soaking in the beauty of nature. It's comforting somehow. It reinforces the female factor in the balance of the universe.

Now you know why nature is considered feminine . . . don't ever underestimate the power of a WOMAN!

You, too, can become one of those women who commands attention. Even if you had given up on the idea previously, it's not too late. It's never too late! Because, remember, **It's Your Turn!** You may have to dig down deep to find that powerfully sexy YOU, but she's there, still. You just have to reintroduce yourself to her. Become one. And shine brighter than ever before!

Like John Mayer says in his song *No Such Thing*, "I like to think the best of me is still hiding up my sleeve!"

And now for something completely different . . . .

The World of Sensuality and Decadence

It's also time for you to start enjoying the sensual things in life. I'm sure you already have a list of your own, but also consider these indulgences:

- Wine and sparkling wine (unless you have a problem with overindulgence, then sparkling cider)
- Chocolate, chocolate, and more chocolate, especially dark
- Fresh-cut flowers
- Music
- Flowering plants and herb plants
- Fragrant flowers--stop and stick your nose in them--the scent will change your day!
- Luxurious eye cream
- StriVectin Hand Cream--miracle!
- Bold flavors and colors
- Candles, especially on your work desk
- Art
- Water, whether drinking it or floating in it
- A nap--totally rejuvenating!
- A walk in Nature
- Truffle Pâté--try it with a piece of petite sweet pickle, really!
- A fabulous big brimmed hat and designer sunglasses that make you feel like a movie star

- The feeling of sun on your skin
- Spa treatments
- Endless lobster with butter and lemon (try a little tabasco sauce in the butter. It will blow your mind!)

There are so many things out there that qualify as being sensual and decadent. It's all about your personal taste. And *now* it's your turn to choose what you like, not what someone else would like. How great is that? **BE SELFISH!**

Treating yourself on a daily basis helps you stay motivated. If you feel like you are deserving of something pleasurable, which you are, you are more likely to stick with your new goals and direction. These indulgences are affordable enough that you can enjoy at least one of them a day. And like I've said before, "You are worth it! It's Your Turn, Dammit!"

To make the most of your transition, you have to embrace this newfound freedom. You have to be selfish in your decisions about what you want. You have to be committed to making your transformation successful. And, remember, life is too short for regrets!

Your SELFISH Declarations:

"I am a **SELFISH WOMAN** who takes care of myself first, because **I'M WORTH IT!**"
"I am the **LEADING LADY of MY OWN LIFE!**"

"It's My Turn!"

Your SELFISH Action Steps:

1. Give yourself permission to be Selfish.
2. Don't feel guilty for putting yourself first. If you start feeling guilty, snap out of it and shout to the sky, "I deserve it, damn it!"
3. When you start "hearing" those old tapes about putting yourself at the end of the line of needs, *change that channel.* Listen to the new tape that says, "I'm worth it! It's my turn!"
4. Don't breathe life into your old story by talking about it. Choose a *new* story for your *new* future.

5. Start researching what is involved to begin the career of your dreams. Set a date for change, make a plan, and work the plan. Do it now. Every step you take in that direction is just as important as the goal itself. This will be very empowering. You will be able to see the light.
6. Enjoy at least one thing a day that you consider sensuous, or decadent. Make sure you savor the moment. YOU deserve it!
7. Thank God for your New Life!

Step Two

E Is for ENERGETIC LIFESTYLE

It is time to focus on energizing your lifestyle. Tapping into the energy that makes you vibrant, vivacious, and dynamic.

But you can't achieve this if you have no energy!

You've been living an existence that has sucked the life out of you. Now is the time to get that life back! To get back to the land of the living!

One thing you need to know is that you can *make* your own stress, and you can *eliminate* your own stress. Worrying about things can create stress. Exercising can eliminate stress.

It is important for you to start being physically active. You'll get those endorphins going, making you feel better. The results will be more energy for your mind and body, not to mention a better night's sleep, and your skin will look fresher and younger.

And if you want to get to looking hot and sexy, you do it for yourself, not anyone else. People come and go, but you will always have YOU. And that is who *you* need to focus on. You are worth it, and now is the time to start.

I will:

- help you achieve a healthy body,
- show you how to dial exercise into your life,
- make it as fun as possible, and
- encourage you to enjoy your community and get involved.

I will not:

- feed you unrealistic expectations to look like a super model on a magazine cover. Even super models don't look like their magazine covers. Enough said.
- encourage you to start an exercise program without consulting your doctor to assess your current physical health.

My World

I have chosen to live in the "Big Babe" world. That's what I call the world of *real* women.

- The women like you and me who will never be the size of a model without going anorexic. Boring!
- The women who have had children, and our body has never forgiven us.
- The women who just want to be healthy and happy with their true body size.

That's all! That's not too much to ask, right? But this requires changing our mind-set. Changing the way we think about and use food and exercise. Our goal is to be healthy and happy!

I got the term "Big Babe" from Mary Carillo, the sports commentator. That's how she describes the world of women's tennis. Most of the players now are tall, *really* tall. But my take on "Big Babe" is to embrace the *realistic* you. The body you can accomplish and be proud of. Not an unrealistic image that would require damaging our health to achieve. Health is the key word here.

There is an important balance between the amount of calories you take in and the amount of energy you expend. It's that easy! You need to burn more than you ingest. There you have the secret of maintaining a healthy weight. Any more questions? (I know, what about the food side of the equation? I'll cover that in the *Step Four "F is for Feeding Your Body."*)

Of all the different "diets" out there, the common thread is burning more calories than you eat and getting most of those calories from fruits and vegetables. That's it! That is the basic philosophy. Most diets promote that you eat clean, lean, unprocessed, and natural foods. If processed foods are part of a diet program, and you know which ones I'm talking about, then that company is just trying to sell you something!

You don't have to "buy" any specific diet, you just have to change the way you think, shop, and cook. And it will cost far less than buying one of those diet programs.

Now here is where the exercising comes in. I don't mean one hour a day, every day. *I* don't have time *I* want to spend that way. If you do, and want to, then your results will happen faster. But I do mean at least four times per week, preferably five hours total per week. Whether you choose walking, jogging, cycling, rowing, tennis, yoga, or a combination thereof, pick something that you like doing. And shake it up when possible. Also, do more than one activity in a week when possible. It keeps your body from getting comfortable with one constant form of exercise.

Side note: Remember, our goal is to be healthy, not skinny! Skinny does not mean healthy, just grumpy! Also, if you have any health issues or physical limitations, please consult your physician before starting an exercise program. Better safe than sorry!

Load up your iPod with music that has the same beat as the pace you want to keep. Also, download audiobooks or language lessons that you can listen to while you are exercising. The time goes by so much faster, and you are learning something new at the same time. That's my kind of multitasking!

Another beneficial use of your exercise time is reinforcing your affirmations. I cover affirmations in *Step Six - S is for Success.* You can get some intense focus time on what you want to bring into your life at the same time you are contributing to your health. The intensity of your dreams and the intensity of your exercise can work together to bring your desires into your life. Say your affirmations as if they are already your reality. And thank God for them. The more consistent your focus, more quickly you will bring these desires into your reality. Don't underestimate the power of your thoughts! Again, this is the Universal Law of Attraction. It works!

Figure out what is the best time during the day for your exercise. The time that is the easiest to dial into your schedule. Keep in mind, the earlier, the better. That keeps your metabolism burning at a higher rate for the next few hours, which burns more calories during the day. Score!

The later in the day you exercise, the more likely it is to affect your sleep. If it's too late in the day, you may have trouble shutting down. And sleep is too important to your overall health to mess with.

If you think it will be more fun to go with a friend, try to find one that will commit. Even if that friend can only go part time, it will be a nice addition to your routine.

Cross-training is also great. Cross-training is training in two or more sports in order to improve fitness and performance.

- It keeps the fun factor alive.
- It keeps your body from getting comfortable with one certain exercise.
- It targets more areas of your body in less time.

Remember, every extra bit of energy you exert is more calories burned in a day. The older we get, the more important that becomes. That includes running up your stairs instead of walking, not parking right by the front door of the grocery store, you know what I mean. When you are awake, be awake and active. When you are tired, sleep. Don't mix the two.

Also, never underestimate the benefit of the power nap. I am a firm believer in power naps. They are so refreshing. And they don't cost a thing.

When you are exercising, it is really important to get enough sleep. Your body needs time to repair the tissue damage and build the muscle we are going for. This is natural, and good. Eight hours a night. Really! Make it happen. No excuses. You need it more than you know. Especially now.

If you aren't used to exercising, start with walking. Take the dog, wear sunscreen--especially on your neck--grab your hat and sunglasses, crank up the tunes, and go!

I highly recommend a Polar Heart Rate Monitor. Ingenious gadget. Keeps track of your heart rate, your heart beat range to stay within, how long you go, how fast you go, and how many calories you burn. You get instant gratification knowing how many calories you've burned. It's motivating. It also keeps an ongoing record of your exercising, if you wear it, of course.

You also need to start lifting weights. I mean hand weights. Go to a sporting goods store and buy 5-pound and 8-pound hand weights, and 1 1/2-pound wrist/ankle weights. And to be clear, each hand will use a 5- or 8-pound weight, and each wrist/ankle weight is 1 1/2 pounds. I encourage using these only in your hands. This saves wear and tear on your knees, hips, and lower back.

Also, get a stability ball and a 6-pound weight ball. That's it. You don't have to pay for a club membership unless you want to. For about $90 total you can have all the equipment you need for weight training, and you only have to pay for it once. Save that money you would spend on a gym membership, and . . . get your hair done professionally every month. Perfect financial trade-off!

My method of exercising is for the home. I'm not one to join a gym. For me it takes too much time, from getting ready to exercise, to travel time, to workout time, to showering and getting dressed, then getting on with my day. Plus, I like to walk the dog at the same time, be outside, get my sun allotment for the day, and cut down on the total turnaround time. It works better for my life.

You need to incorporate exercise into your life however it works best for you. And if that means belonging to a gym, do it. I'm for whatever keeps you motivated. That's what is most important. Adapt this philosophy into your lifestyle so that you can maintain consistency. At a gym you can always consult a trainer for the proper use of the machines. Otherwise, I will be providing you with basic techniques.

Now for Something Really Important! BREATHING!

You need to control your breathing for the most efficient workout. Breath control can keep your heart from blowing the top of your head off!

At the beginning, it will be hard to control your breath. You might think your lungs just can't do it. But you can train your lungs to expand beyond your normal breathing range. The lungs can hold far more air than we normally use. Twenty to thirty percent of our lung capacity is the normal usage. But athletes train themselves to breathe more deeply and efficiently for longer endurance and better performance. You can, too.

While you are exercising, be it walking, jogging, or interval training, focus on your breathing. Your goal here is to breathe in through your nose and out through your mouth. Breathe in through your nose for five counts and out through your mouth for three counts.

When you get winded, you tend to pant. Don't! You could hyperventilate. This is when you really need to regain control of your breathing. Focus on breathing in through your nose for five, out of your mouth for three. Keep at it until you are back under control. If you are really struggling, make it four counts in and two counts out until you can resume the five in, three out pace.

Breath control can also lower your heart rate when it is beating too rapidly. If your heart is beating too fast, breathe in for the count of eight through your nose, then out for the count of eight through your mouth. Close your eyes and concentrate if you need to. Keep at it until you have complete control of your breathing rate; then maintain a consistent rate for at least a minute.

When weightlifting, you need to breathe opposite of what you would think. Breathe out as you lift and in as you lower. Take a deep breath before you start, then out through your mouth as you lift, for the same count as you are lifting. Then breathe in through your nose as you lower the weights, again for the same count as you lower. Out as you lift for four counts, in as you lower for four counts. This will help you keep your torso tight and your shoulders down. Practice and focus.

Same with squats, breathe out when you bend your legs and in when you raise back up. Out through your mouth, in through your nose.

And Let's Not Forget Water!

Drinking enough water on a daily basis is paramount to clean, healthy living. It improves you circulation, "washes out" your system, and removes the toxins from your body.

A continuous flow of water in your system keeps everything moving along. Keeps your muscles cleaned out, your cells cleaned out, your skin cleaned out, your colon cleaned out . . . see where I'm going with this?

Especially when exercising, water flushes out the toxins that are released from our fat cells when they start getting smaller. Toxins from our food and environment are stored in our fat cells. Same with animals, which is why I say only eat "lean" proteins. Don't eat fat from animals if possible. And if you do, make sure it is from an organically raised animal. Our livers don't need any more toxins to deal with.

Dr. Jonny Bowden, the famous nutritionist, suggests in his book *The 150 Healthiest Foods on Earth* that you divide your body weight by two, and that is how many ounces of water you should drink a day. For example, 170 pounds divided by two is 85; 85 divided by eight is 10.62. So you would need to drink at least ten and one half 8 ounce glasses of water a day. Now divide that by how many hours a day you are awake, and you know how often you should have a glass of water in your hand. Get the idea?

I recommend getting a water filtration system in your house. It's cheaper over the long run than buying bottled water. And you can control the quality of water you are drinking, using for cooking, and making ice cubes. Also, get one of those stainless steel containers that doesn't affect your water. Glass will also do. Find one that will fit in your purse and keep it on you at all times. Make sure you fill it with fresh water often.

You just have to get in the habit of drinking water. No matter where you are, you have water on you. It will keep you full, increase your energy level, keep your synapses popping, and, yes, keep you going to the bathroom often. But it's a small sacrifice for all the fabulous benefits!

Exercise Phases

I'm going to describe phases of exercise based on fitness levels. You read them and decide which one describes your level. Then work from there to the next level, and so on. Also consider which phase works with the amount of time you can allocate for exercise. Yes, your goal is to get to the highest level possible, but be realistic about what you can dial into your life. That way you are more likely to be consistent with your exercise.

Also, you can make compensations for a limited schedule. If you only have 30 minutes to walk that day, or you are walking with someone who can't walk as fast or as long as you can, add hand weights. One and a half pounds up to three-pound hand weights are good. Any more than that gets hard to hold and can cause back or hip pain dare you misstep.

Many of us do not live in a city where we can walk to most places or ride a bike like in Paris or New York City. We live in cities that require cars to get where we need to go and carry what we need to carry. So, we have to make an effort to dial exercise into our daily lives.

With our goal being health and happiness, don't get obsessed with exercising because of the way it can make you look. Create a healthy balance mentally and physically so that you don't neglect other important parts of your life.

Phase I

This is the absolute beginning. You have never exercised before, and you need to know where to start.

- Begin with walking 30 minutes a day, four to five times per week,
- Focus on your breathing, in through nose for count of five, out through mouth for three,
- Increase your protein intake and your water intake daily.

Phase II

- Begin brisk walking 30 to 45 minutes a day, four to five times per week.
- Start incorporating interval training (see below).
- Using 3- to 5 pound hand weights, follow Weightlifting 101 below, three times per week, with at least one day of no weightlifting in between.
- Do as many repetitions as you can until the muscle feels tired, but only do two sets of each exercise.
- Increase your protein and water intake daily.

Phase III

- Begin power walking 45 to 60 minutes a day, four to five times per week.
- Incorporate interval training (see below).
- Using 5- to 8 pound hand weights, follow Weightlifting 101 below, three times per week, with at least one day of no weightlifting in between.
- Complete three sets of each exercise; when 5 pound weights become easy to lift, move up to the 8 pound weights.
- Keep your water intake high--it flushes out the toxins.

Phase IV

- You are Superwoman!
- You don't need me!

Treadmill Tips

Treadmills are great to have if you use them properly. The freedom to work out no matter what the weather is fabulous. Not to mention that it doesn't matter what you look like!

It's important that you don't let yourself use the incline function. Tempting as it is, the act of walking fast at an incline on a narrow belt is dangerous. It's too easy to misstep and land on the sides of the platform. At a high speed, you can hurt your lower back, and that's if you don't fly off the back of the machine like a rag doll!

You can get just as much or more of a challenge with hand weights instead of the incline. This is where wrist/ankle weights come in. One to two pounds for each hand is perfect. Wear them on your wrist, not on your ankles. It frees your hands to be able to grab on to the railing of the treadmill if you get tired or unbalanced. The freedom of the grab is good.

If you wear the weights on your ankles, you are more likely to injure your knees and lower back. Not good! It hurts!

You can also wear your sauna suit (discussed below) on the treadmill. Then step outside before you take it off. It will be filled with sweat that you don't want on your floor inside.

Don't forget your heart-rate monitor. It will keep up with your statistics for your workout.

Remember to warm up for about five minutes at 2.5 miles per hour, then increase your speed to between 3.5 and 4.0. That speed should eventually bring your heart rate up to 135, which is our target.

It may take your heart rate a while to get up to the 130 to 145 zone. You may have to increase your speed to a light run for a few minutes to get your heart rate up sooner, which is what I do. Hold on to the railing if you need to for balance. Safety is the key! Then slow your speed back down to between 3.5 and 4.0 miles per hour to stay around the 135 heart-rate zone.

If your heart rate gets above 145, slow down your speed until your heart rate gets back down to the 135 area. We don't want to burn muscle, just fat.

Now, this is where interval training, which is also discussed below, can come in. Jog on the treadmill for one minute, then slow back down to a fast paced walk for five minutes. Then repeat for a total of at least six jog and six walk intervals over the course of your 45 minutes of exercise.

Whatever form of exercising on the treadmill you do, always end your exercise period with a cool down. For the last five minutes, at least, slow down your pace to 2.5 miles per hour to bring your heart rate down slowly. This will keep you from getting light headed or dizzy from stopping too quickly. If you can, start your five minute cool down after your 45 minute period.

As far as the exercises below, pick the ones that you have an interest in or need for. Doing all of these exercises every time would take up way too much of your life, so choose the ones you think you need.

Remember, this is for your health, not to "move mountains!"

Weightlifting 101 Tips

- Only lift weights after you have done your cardio exercise. Your muscles need to be warmed up before you lift weights so you won't tear a muscle or hurt yourself.
- Have a glass of fresh water at the ready.
- Keep your knees slightly bent, feet about shoulder width apart.
- Tighten your torso when lifting weights.
- Keep your body in alignment as much as possible to prevent pulling a muscle, especially in your back and neck.
- Lifting weights slowly works the muscles more completely, lifting fast is not as effective, so slowly for the count of four up, and slowly for four down.
- You don't want to build more muscle than you can maintain easily--it will become flabby if not maintained. This is why I don't suggest hand weights more than 8 pounds. If you are younger, stronger, and disciplined, then go for it.

Upper Body

Shoulder focus
For the front and sides of your shoulders:

- Stand with feet shoulder width apart, back straight, knees slightly bent, shoulders down.
- A weight in each hand, start with 5 pounds.
- Begin with your weights and wrists facing your thighs.
- Elbows slightly bent, focus on keeping your shoulders down the whole time.
- Lift weights slowly to shoulder height, breathing out of your mouth for a count of four.
- Then slowly lower weights back down to thighs, breathing in your nose for a count of four.
- Now move the weights around to the outer side of your thighs.
- Slowly lift weights from your sides out and up to shoulder height, breathing out for a count of four.
- Slowly lower weights back down to your side, breathing in for a count of four.

- Do 10 to 12 repetitions in that order.
- Drink water.

Arnold Press (Also for Shoulders)

- Sit on a stability ball, back straight, 5-pound weights in hands, knees apart for balance.
- Put arms out to side, elbows inline with your shoulders at 90-degree angles from floor, hands at ear level.
- Slowly press the weights directly up until your arms straighten, breathing out for a count of four, letting the weights touch at their ends.
- Push your shoulders down at the same time.
- Slowly lower weights back to beginning position, breathing in for a count of four.
- Repeat 12 to 18 times.
- Drink water.
- Sitting on the stability ball also tightens your core muscles.
- Now move to biceps curls.
- Drink water.

Biceps focus

- Stand with feet shoulder width apart, back straight, knees slightly bent.
- Put 5-pound weights in each hand.
- With arms straight down by your sides, open wrists facing forward.
- Keep elbows tight to your sides.
- Bend at the elbows and raise the weights slowly up to the shoulders, breathing out for a count of four.
- Slowly lower, keeping the elbows tight to your sides, breathing in for a count of four.
- Do 15 to 20 repetitions. When 5 pounds gets easy, move up to 8 pounds.
- Drink water.

Triceps focus

- Put 5-pound weights in each hand.
- Feet shoulder width apart, knees slightly bent.
- Elbows by your side, and bent to a 90-degree angle from the floors.

- Lean your body over to a 45-degree angle, back flat, with knees slightly bent and elbows lifted toward the ceiling behind you. Your elbows should bend like hinges on a puppet.
- With wrists facing each other, slowly extend the weights backward until your arms are straight and lifting towards the ceiling behind you, breathing out for a count of four.
- Then slightly lift the weights higher, toward the ceiling, feeling the triceps muscle tighten.
- Slowly return the weights to the beginning position, breathing in for a count of four.
- Repeat 12 to 15 times.
- Drink water.

You should do one set of shoulders, one set of biceps, and one set of triceps as a sequence. Then go back to your second set of shoulders, biceps, and triceps, until you have completed three sets. This method gives your muscles a short rest in between sets, which you will soon see that you need. Your goal is to exhaust your muscles with each set.

Also, to shake things up, occasionally change the order of the lifting so your muscles don't get used to the same thing over and over.

Torso

Core focus

First exercise:

- Lie with your back flat on a padded floor, carpet, mat, whatever.
- Bend knees, feet flat on the floor and slightly apart.
- Holding the 6-pound exercise ball over your stomach, as you slowly lift your upper torso off the ground, lift the ball up and over your knees, exhaling as you raise your upper body.
- Make sure your feet do not come up off the floor.
- The stronger you get, the farther you can reach past your knees.
- Slowly lower back down to the lying position, inhaling as you lower.
- Repeat for three sets of 15, resting for 10 to 20 seconds between sets.
- Drink water.

Second exercise:

- Now lie on your back, flat on the floor with the stability ball under your heels, body straight.
- Tighten your buttocks and lift your hips off the ground, making a straight bridge from your shoulders to your feet, no knee bend.
- Balance your body, trying not to let your feet roll around on the ball.
- Keep your torso as tight as possible to prevent shaking.
- The stronger your core gets, the more steady you can keep your feet.
- Hold this lift for a slow count of five, then lower.
- Repeat for three sets of 12 to 15 times, resting 10 to 20 seconds between sets.
- Drink water.

Tucus focus

- Squats with the stability ball: Proper squats are done by standing with feet shoulder width apart. Bending at knees and hips and leaning torso slightly forward for balance but still upright, lower the torso as far down as you can by bending the knees, then rise back up to standing position. Feel as if a string is attached to your head and the ceiling and is pulling you up and down in a straight line.
- Now to incorporate the ball: with your back up against a wall, place the stability ball between your lower back and the wall.
- Leaning back into the ball, squat down so that your knees are at a 90-degree angle to the floor, rolling the ball down your back, ball against the wall, your weight on your heels, not the ball of your foot.
- Hold for five counts, then slowly raise back up.
- Repeat for three sets of 15 to 20 times.
- Drink water.
- Side note: For more core work, use your stability ball as a chair, either for your computer chair or just for watching TV. The act of staying balanced on the ball works your core muscles, and it's a no-brainer.

Legs

Toning Exercise

- Power walking will begin the toning of your legs (power walking is explained later in this chapter).
- To combine exercises for time efficiency, you can incorporate squats with your shoulder work.
- Referencing the *shoulder focus* above, bend your knees, lowering your body to a squat, for the same amount of time it takes to lift hand weights to shoulder level.
- Then lower the hand weights back down to your thighs while straightening your legs.
- The lower you can squat without sticking your butt way out in back and throwing off your alignment, the more beneficial the exercise.

Calf focus

- To define your calf muscles, stand with the ball of your feet on the edge of a stair, lowering your heels down to the lower step as far as they will go, having enough of the foot on the upper stair to prevent sliding off completely.
- Hold onto the railing and the wall for balance.
- This position should be held for at least a minute to stretch the Achilles tendon and the plantar fascia in your feet.
- Then raise your heels as high as you can so that you are standing completely on the ball of your feet, like a ballet dancer.
- Feel the calf muscle tighten as much as possible.
- Then lower all the way back down to the stretching position.
- Repeat 10 to 12 times, three sets with a minute rest in between sets.
- End by holding the lowered stretching position for at least three minutes.

Goal and Focus

Your goal is to be successful. Your goal is three sets of all these exercises. If you must, start with two sets and work your way up to three sets, three times a week. Also, some of us have parts of our body that don't need more definition. For me, it's my calves. The walking keeps my calves defined enough. That's why I say work on the exercises your body needs.

Your focus is to see results. Your focus is to feel firm, tight, and strong. You are going to *feel* so fabulous when you don't *feel* yourself jiggling when you walk. You are going to be proud when someone touches your arm and comments on how tight and strong it feels. I'm telling you, **it's great!**

I work out Monday through Friday, with weightlifting on Monday, Wednesday, and Friday. You always need at least 48 hours between weightlifting sessions. Your muscle tissue breaks down every time the muscle is used to lift weights. It takes at least 48 hours for your muscle tissue to heal. When the muscles recover from lifting weights, they also build more tissue in their recovery, which builds stronger muscles, which burns more calories, which is our goal. More muscle tissue burns more calories in a resting state, not to mention an active state, which, again, is our goal. I average four days of cardio. Sometimes I work out four times a week and sometimes five. But I lift weights only three times a week, and sometimes on a weekend day to make up for a weekday that I was busy. Be flexible.

If you don't have enough time in one particular day to complete all the exercises, maybe do the upper body every other day and the lower body on the in-between days. Whatever works for you will make you successful.

Make sure that you drink a lot of water when you are exercising. Not just during the activity, but all day long. Remember, at least ten 8-ounce glasses a day. The muscles need that clean water flushing the toxins out of your body. You will also not be as sore in the beginning if you keep the water flowing.

Another goal is to build on success. For every day that you work out, that is a successful day. For every day of the week that you work out, that is a successful week. You are setting a habit of success. This is very empowering. And, again, you are focusing on success. What you focus on expands . . . . There you have it. You are successfully accomplishing your goal!

Stretching

When your body is not used to exercising, it can get sore. Stretching your muscles when you are sore can ease the pain. The stretch helps release the stiffness that is causing the discomfort. It also can help keep the muscles from tightening up after being exercised.

Remember, you only want to stretch your muscles after they have been warmed up. This prevents possible pulling or tearing of the muscle fiber if cold and stiff. When you begin your workout, do some form of cardio for at least 5-10 minutes before you stop and stretch. Stretching after your workout will also help keep your circulation and blood flow running free and clear. It will help prevent your muscles from tightening up, and it will help keep you from getting as sore as you would without stretching.

Start with a gentle stretch of your muscles by lowering your upper body and touching the floor. Just let your body hang. Your body will naturally lower as your muscles stretch out. No bouncing, just hang there. Eventually grab your ankles, pull your face to your legs, and hold.

Also, raising your hands over your head and then over to each side and forward with a flat back will slowly stretch your torso, back, hips, and legs. Again, don't bounce or force any stretching when sore. Not good. Even just walking for 20 minutes will increase your blood flow and flush out the soreness. If you are new at exercising, this sore phase will pass. Not to worry. Just keep on keeping on.

In-Home Sauna

For those of us that don't have a sauna at home, here's how to clean out your system the natural way.

Get one of those plastic sauna suits. They may cost $10. At least once a week, when time permits, wear both pieces of the suit while you are doing your cardio workout.

Make sure you are using your heart-rate monitor when you wear the sauna suit. You want to be aware of your heart rate so you can avoid overheating. Slow your pace down if you have to. Keep your heart rate in your normal target zone, between 130 and 145.

You will purge your system of excess fluid, removing impurities at the same time you exercise. Remember, though, that it is even more important to drink water while you are sweating. The fresh water encourages the flushing of your cells and your system. Your skin will also get a cleansing.

It's like sitting in a sauna to sweat but still being able to accomplish your cardio at the same time. (I can't help multitasking whenever possible.)

If you can dial in this cleansing a couple of times a week, you will keep your water weight at bay. And your skin will start to glow. Make sure your skin is clean before you start this process, though. Your pores will open and as the sweat comes out of your skin, it will bring out the impurities with it. You don't want makeup blocking the cleansing process.

Word to the wise: If you are anything like me, your sweat will drip out the bottom of the suit. Make sure you are prepared with towels to catch it coming out of your sleeves. If you are on your treadmill at home, be prepared for the sweat to drip onto the floor. And don't even think about taking the suit off anyplace other than in the shower or outside! I'm sure you know what I mean. It's a mess! You will want to rinse the suit out each time anyway, so the shower is the best bet. Also, don't wear your best athletic shoes when using the sauna suit. They will be drenched with sweat and hard to clean. Duly noted!

That said, the cleansing benefits are worth it. Your skin and waistline will thank you!

Benefits of Exercise

The benefits of physical exercise are endorphins, energy, bright eyes, bright skin, sharp mind, great sleep, empowerment, positive attitude, slimmer body, and a peaceful soul. And it is inexpensive to boot. Not to mention the health benefits of keeping your stress level down and many illnesses at bay. Need I say more?

I don't want to have to spend time and energy worrying about how many calories I've taken in or burned each day. It's exhausting, not to mention time consuming. It's also stressful and negative. I want to use that energy to feel better about myself, not worse. That's why eating clean and lean and living an active lifestyle are so important.

If you focus on the negative, you set the tone for your results. If you focus on becoming healthy and strong, you are focusing on success!

The Power Walk

According to Wikipedia, power walking is "walking at a speed at the upper end of the natural walking gait." If you are on a treadmill, you would be in the 3.8-4.2 mph range. This is the speed where walking and jogging are almost equally effective, but with less joint impact.

The difference in walking and jogging is that with walking, one foot will be in contact with the ground at all times. The similarities are the exaggerated arm swing and the health benefits.

Now, when you exercise, it is all about YOU, no one else. No cell phones, no business, no diverting your focus unless it's for fun.

If you have to multitask, do it in your breathing, your awareness, and your enjoyment.

For some of you, exercising will be a new thing. Start slow. And remember, if you have any physical concerns, consult your doctor and alter these suggestions accordingly.

For others, you've probably gone through a period in your life where the last thing you had time for was exercising. You've had enough on your plate to handle with all the changes going on.

Even if you normally exercise, in whatever form that takes, now is the time to be **SELFISH**. Do this for yourself, for your mental and emotional well-being. **It's Your Turn!**

A few tips before you get started:

1. Make sure you have well padded cross-training athletic shoes. If you have trouble with plantar fasciitis, add orthotics and/or gel pads to your heels.
2. Get music on your iPod that has the same beat as the speed you want to walk. That makes it easier to stay at a consistent pace without too much thought. Always have the volume low enough to hear what is going on around you. Safety is the key! You are empowered and in control now. Act like it!
3. The more you control breathing, the easier and longer you can exercise. Breathe in through your nose for a count of five, and out through your mouth for a count of three. Even when you get winded, stay in control of your breathing. In five, out three. Controlled breathing will help keep you from panting and help keep your heart rate at a safe level. If you cannot maintain this breathing pattern, slow down until you can!
4. If the temperature outside is 80 degrees or hotter, take water with you. Don't run the risk of getting overheated. Also, be relentless with the sunscreen. From the base of your neck up, use at least 45 SPF zinc oxide sunscreen. SkinCeuticals has a great one. And a hat or visor is a must!
5. Use a heart-rate monitor. Just go buy one, and use it each time. The monitor will keep you informed of how efficiently you are working out. You want to stay within a "fat burning" zone, unless you are interval training. The optimal zone is between 130 and 145 beats per minute. The monitor tells you what your heart rate is, based on your physique. Enter all your stats into the monitor, and it will be personalized for your body and age. If your heart rate gets higher than 145, slow down.

Get your breathing back under control and that will help lower your heart rate. Getting above your zone only burns the energy from your muscle, not from your fat. Muscle--good! Fat--bad! We don't want to burn the muscle we are working so hard to make!

6. Don't forget to check with your doctor if you aren't already exercising to make sure you are healthy enough to start.

As for length of time, your goal is 45 minutes to an hour, four to five times per week. If for some reason you can only do 30 minutes on a particular day, go for it. Anything is better than nothing! But aim for 45 minutes, four times per week minimum.

If you will power walk instead of run, you will get all the cardio benefits without the wear and tear on your body. Big plus!

Drink water! Drink water! Drink water! You must stay hydrated.

When you are walking, make sure you know what is going on around you. Safety is the key! Take your dog, if you have one.

Also, choose a route that is aesthetically pleasing: a neighborhood with big houses, a local park with lots of trees and shade. Whatever you have access to, make sure you don't get bored visually. Change your route occasionally. This will increase your enjoyment.

Try to tighten your abdominal muscles while you walk. It will take awhile to do it automatically, but the more you tighten your stomach muscles, the firmer your torso will become. Also, bend your arms at the elbows and pump them with each step. You will burn more calories this way.

After the first 5 to 10 minutes of your walk, stop and stretch your calf muscles and Achilles tendons by putting the ball of your feet on the top of a curb, and lower your heels down to the street level. It's easier to do this leaning on a mailbox or light pole. Hold the stretch for at least 2 minutes, and don't bounce. This will also stretch the plantar fascia, which will help prevent foot pain.

If your lower back starts hurting, it may be because your hamstrings need to be stretched out. With your knees slightly bent, lean over to touch the ground. Let your body hold that position for at least a minute or two to stretch the hamstrings. Again, no bouncing. You can also stand with one leg crossed over the other, then lean over to touch the ground. Let your body hang there. It will slowly lower as your hamstring stretches out. Then change legs and do it again.

Another reason for lower back pain could be weak stomach muscles. Make sure that you are tightening your abdominal muscles when you are walking. The more you tighten you abdominal muscles in a day, the stronger your core will become, faster. This is where you will benefit from the core exercises mentioned above. Now get back to the rest of your power walk.

And did I say to drink water?

Toward the end of your power walk, give yourself at least 5 minutes to cool down. Slow down your pace, so that your body can naturally cool down without stopping completely. Cooling down slowly keeps your circulation flowing without an abrupt stop in activity. It can keep you from getting light-headed. It also can prevent blood pooling in the muscle tissue, which promotes soreness. You want the toxins that have been stirred up and ready for removal to continue to flow through and out of your system. We don't want those toxins to pool in your muscles. This slower pace allows the body time to remove these toxins from the muscle tissue.

Make sure you use this time with yourself, for yourself! Do your affirmations, work on your current problems, and reinforce your new attitude and approach to life. *What you focus on expands!* Use this time to focus on the NEW YOU!

Remember, with every step that you take forward, you are reinforcing the new direction of your New Life!

Interval Training

Interval training is exercise that alternates between high intensity and lower intensity training. With walking as our example, you would burst into jogging or sprinting for a minute, then slow back down to the fast walking pace for maybe 5 minutes, then burst into the jogging, and back down to the walking. Ideally you want to do this at least five to ten times during your overall 45 minutes, making sure your body has adequately warmed up before the first high intensity period.

A good rule of thumb is the high intensity period should last long enough to get you out of breath, which could be anywhere from 1-5 minutes, depending on what type of exercise you are doing. You want your lower intensity period to be long enough for your heart rate to return to whatever rate is normally for you at the slower period of exertion. Another good rule is to only do the interval training two to three times per week. This will help to prevent burnout.

Internal training is not just for advanced exercisers. It has the same positive effects on beginners, too. Word of caution: According to Walter R. Thompson, professor of exercise science at Georgia State University in Atlanta, if you have certain physical conditions like heart disease, high blood pressure, joint problems, or you are over 60, you should check with your doctor before starting interval training.

Now, back to the positive effects. According to research done at The University of Texas at Austin, the McMaster University in Hamilton, Ontario, and studies published by the *Journal of Applied Physiology*, interval training dramatically improves cardiovascular fitness and raises the body's potential for burning fat.

Cardiovascular fitness is the ability of the heart and lungs to get oxygen to the muscles. This in turn increases your endurance. Interval training promotes the body's cells to burn fat first, before tapping into carbohydrate reserves. It also builds new muscle tissue, which in turn burns more calories even at a resting rate. So, interval training improves your cardiovascular fitness, your endurance, muscle tone, AND raises your body's potential for burning fat. That's what I'm talking about!

Now For More Fun!

Exercise isn't the only way to lead an energetic lifestyle. You need to get out and go! It's time to get out of your comfort zone--your home--and get out *there*--the rest of the world.

Start going to festivals in your city. It can be food festivals, music festivals, marathons, eating contests, hot sauce contests, crazy boat decorating parades, you name it. They are out there. Funky, interesting collections of funky, interesting people.

Look up your city's listings of all the events going on, and pick some. You get out, you see crazy stuff, maybe even meet fun people. Try it.

Join organizations you have an interest in, or passion for, like a food and wine foundation. They offer great tastings, seminars, exciting auctions, and put you in a room with people who share the same interests. You name the passions, and there will be groups out there supporting them.

Be involved with a charity and support a good cause. Everyone should have a charity they support. It's important that we all give back in some way.

A lot of churches have great singles programs. They do anything from getting groups together for dining, dancing, listening to live music, to working on some kind of mission project. This is a great outlet.

Travel clubs and dinner clubs are also good choices. Start taking cooking classes, wine tastings, craft classes. Check out live music venues, concerts in the park, local farmers' markets, cool grocery stores.

Find something you have a passion for and join a group that shares that passion. You will already have built in conversation material. How easy is that?

Your ENERGETIC Declarations:

"I will exercise, live healthy, AND eliminate my own stress."
"I will be more active with my passions in my life!"

"It's My Turn!"

Your ENERGETIC Action Steps:

1. Worrying about things causes stress. Stop making your own stress.
2. Commit to exercising a minimum of four days a week.
3. Commit to lifting weights three times per week.
4. Decide what type of exercise you will stick with and enjoy.
5. Make sure you have the right pair of athletic shoes and maybe a cute little outfit. OK, maybe later on the outfit.
6. Get your iPod loaded with great music, interesting audiobooks, foreign language lessons. Get at it and learn, Baby, learn.
7. Get those shoes on and GO! Just don't forget the sunscreen and sunglasses.
8. Look up the different events going on in your city; pick some and go!
9. Commit to going to two new places a week, whether it's an event or a new restaurant.
10. Join a new interest group that feeds one of your passions. Wine, art, food, charity, just do it. It will be fun. And you will meet new people.
11. Thank God for your New Life!

Step Three

L Is for LAUGHTER

It's all about enjoying life and choosing a positive attitude. Because it ***IS*** your choice.

Attitude is everything! I repeat: **Attitude is everything!**

It's what separates the good from the bad, the strong from the weak, the happy from the sad.

And happiness is a *choice*, not a *result* of circumstances. It is all in your control.

You can dictate the outcome of almost any situation by how you choose to respond to it.

The way you react to what happens to you is ***completely*** in your control. Yes, bad things happen to good people. *Life* happens to everybody! But the way we respond to it reveals our true character.

You can choose to whine and pout, still not changing what's already happened, and make yourself feel miserable. *Or* you can choose to have a positive response to a bad situation, making yourself feel less of a victim and more in control of the outcome. This choice will accelerate your recovery from whatever *life* dishes out.

You will never make a successful recovery from your divorce if you continue to feed energy to that old phase of your life. You are giving it a lifeline that it does *not* deserve! Flip off that life support! Quick!

Continuing to talk about the past keeps you from totally releasing its hold over you. That is not our goal.

Our goal here is to choose to respond to *life* in a positive way. No matter how bad it gets, and you know *exactly* what I'm talking about; **don't** go over to the dark side.

Choose to respond in an honorable, courageous manner. Don't participate in mudslinging, name-calling, and vengeance. It only prolongs your pain and the power the situation has over you. Refuse to perpetuate the negative. And think about it, if we don't lead by example, who will?

Don't get sucked into other people's chaos. They hope you will because it feeds their negative energy and ego. Some people thrive on that. Just don't participate. It's your choice. People like that will continue to pierce you with hateful comments just to get you to engage. Don't bite. Insults are just that. And you insult yourself by even playing along. You are adding fuel to someone else's fire. And does it really matter what they think anymore anyway? I think not! People, and things, only have the power and meaning you assign to them. Otherwise, they are meaning*less*. This is how you take your power back, where it belongs. Again, our goal!

Also, arguing is a waste of time and energy. I'm not talking about discussing, I'm talking about arguing. Just don't participate. Arguing promotes negativity and hostility. And honestly, if arguing with someone will change your mind about something, then you weren't committed to your opinion enough to be arguing in the first place. And trying to change your EX's mind in this situation is just not going to happen. Trust me!

Remember, don't give your *old life* that power over you anymore. Those days are over! You are now a **SELFISH WOMAN**.

Unfortunately, this *new* attitude on life doesn't shield you from the rest of the emotional world completely. You will still get mud slung at you or the occasional shrapnel piercing from someone else's chaos. But you are now better equipped for handling the situation with wisdom and grace, not from your *old* battered and bruised self, but from your *new*, well-balanced self. And this ***IS*** one of your goals.

There is something else that needs to be discussed here. Don't self-impose feelings of guilt, inadequacy, or idiocy. Those are feelings that you put on yourself. You are the only one who can accept those feelings. No one else can make you feel them. Only you. Again, it's your choice. And as we all know, other people will try their damnedest!

It comes back to your making positive choices for your life. Choosing to participate or not to participate. Choosing how you are going to respond to what happens to you. Choosing how you are going to feel based on what is best for you, not what someone else wants you to do or feel. You have the final choice.

Once you understand this concept, your whole world changes. Your whole perception of life is more positive. Your feeling of personal power radiates, which is another one of our goals!

Laughter

Chances are you're not laughing much right now. That's not good. Laughter gives you a burst of positive energy, breaks through that dark cloud looming overhead, and makes your heart feel good. It releases that knot that is so often in your chest.

Laughter makes you right with the world again, and is hugely important when your goal is to have a positive attitude and enjoy life.

Laughter also has health benefits. Paul Antokolsky, who conducts the Laughter Therapy Group, says that "with laughter, you're getting oxygen into all the cells in your body, which is something we need for energy and vitality." "Laughter can help to lower blood pressure and cholesterol, strengthen the immune system, reduce physical tension and relieve emotional stress." (http://www.laughterforhealth.com/index.html.) It also stimulates chemical production in the brain that lowers anxiety and tension, which naturally makes you feel better.

You would be amazed how many things really are funny that happen in a day. Make it a point to look for the positive, comical things in everyday life. If you can't find any, then you are taking life way too seriously!

Here are some rules to live by:

- Dance whenever possible, with total abandon. Pretend no one is watching!
- Surround yourself with positive people. Positive attitudes are contagious, as are negative ones.
- Enjoy good music, good friends, good food, and good wine. These things improve the quality of life and should never be wasted.
- Listen to the birds, enjoy the warmth of the sun, and soak up some nature every day.
- Have a source of running water around you, whether it is a fountain on a table, on the deck, or from a pool. The soothing sounds of water are hypnotic and peaceful.

And on the flip side:

- Bad things happen to everyone. How you choose to respond shows your true character. Make positive choices.
- Don't tolerate the negatively selfish people. There is never an excuse for that kind of behavior. Stay away!
- You cannot love someone to health. You cannot fix them or change them. Don't even bother.

Even after you adopt this new philosophy of life, negative things will still happen. You will wake up one morning, everything is fine. Then you'll receive a phone call, and it's a flash back to your *old life.*

You can't keep that stuff from happening, but you can choose how you will respond to it. Now you have new tools and skills to handle "bad news" in a more positive manner. If you have truly embraced being a **SELFISH WOMAN** in all of it's positive aspects, it will be much easier to handle these new challenges. You don't have to get sucked back down into the darkness you used to live in. You now know that you can take it. You are stronger, wiser, and calmer. You can handle anything. It won't kill you, like it used to. It is still tiring to deal with negative situations, but with each occurrence, it will get easier. You will get stronger. Just remember, *this too will pass.*

Now back to fun stuff. People are attracted to positive people. The positive energy is infectious. And if we want to make this world a happier, more peaceful place, we have to lead and teach by example.

Cynical, negative energy is just as infectious. Stay away from people that exude those vibes. They will only bring you back down to the level you are trying to escape from. Don't go back there. Black hole--never good.

Stop listening to bad news on TV. Stop reading the paper. Stop opening your financial statement, unless of course that's your livelihood, until you have totally embraced a positive attitude on life.

You would be amazed how all of those negative messages insidiously infiltrate your psyche. You may not have thought about it, but all those news stories or stock losses eat away at your attempt to be positive. Even if just for a month, stop listening, reading, or participating in anything negative, if possible. Especially if you were one of those cynical, negative people to start with. You really don't need to be reminded of how you used to be an active part of that attitude. Again, it's time to shed this! Unless you are more comfortable existing in that negative world . . . If so, stop reading this book, and go on with your day.

Gossiping about people, always thinking the worst of someone, blaming everyone else for what happens to you--this is what we are *not* going to participate in anymore. It is not our place to judge others. We have our hands full of our own regrets. Would you want someone to think the worst of you? Especially when they don't have all the facts? I've had enough of that to last a lifetime.

You have to accept the fact that more times than not we have the final say on what happens to us. You can keep letting someone mistreat you, or you can stop it. You can continue to feel like the victim, or you can change your situation. You have that power. Use it. Only you can choose the feeling you are going to accept.

Time to Enjoy Life

It's time to start enjoying the rest of your life. It's time to do those things you've always wanted to do but let yourself feel guilty for doing. It's time to do those things that are just for you, like traveling, skydiving, zip-lining, having a spa day . . . insert your ideas here.

Since you are now thinking of yourself first and you are making up for lost time, cut loose! Be lavish when you can. You deserve it! You need to do this for yourself because you need to experience firsthand the thrill of it all. And of your own making!

Now is also the time to create your ***Dream Life***. You know, the life you always saw yourself living, but for whatever reason, it never quite happened . . . .

Search your soul . . . what would that ***Dream Life*** look like? What would make you excited to get out of bed each morning, with a big smile on your face? How would you feel? Happy? Positive? Glad to be alive? Yes, yes you would. And you are deserving of that life you've always dreamed of. And the time to achieve that life is now! More on this later.

Life is to be enjoyed. Life is for being the best you can be. Life is for making this world better than it was when you got here.

Now let's get started. Every morning when you wake up, take time to thank God for this new chance at happiness.

A girlfriend reminded me today how important it is to always have something to look forward to. Whether you are planning a trip or trying a new restaurant with friends. It's nice to have something to look forward to. On those days when things are going wrong, you have that carrot dangling in front of you to keep you going. The carrot doesn't have to be big, but it helps. Especially a trip. Try to take one a year. Even if it's just for a weekend. It will do wonders for your outlook. Traveling also feeds your mind and soul. But that will be covered in *Step Five: I Is for INTELLIGENCE.*

Your LAUGHTER Declarations:

"I will choose to respond to life with a positive attitude."
"I will choose the feelings that I will accept."
"I will enjoy life on a daily basis and all it has to offer."
"I will enjoy the funny things around me that happen every day."
"I will leave this world better than it was when I got here."

"It's My Turn!"

Your LAUGHTER Action Steps:

1. Adopt a positive, powerful attitude on life.
2. Look for the humor in the everyday.
3. Let yourself laugh out loud!
4. Choose your outcomes.
5. Choose the feelings that you will accept.
6. Take back your power, and use it wisely.
7. Choose to respond to life in a positive, courageous, and honorable manner.
8. Don't participate in the negativity of other people's chaos.
9. Seek out the happy, fun side of life and appreciate it.
10. Share your enjoyment of life with others.
11. Thank God for your New Life!

Step Four

F Is for FEEDING YOUR BODY

OK, I really don't recognize that person in the mirror looking back at me. I've been known to do a double take. When did I start looking like that? I've been here the whole time. I just didn't know life was leaving its signature on my face. I don't even remember asking for an autograph!

By now we have all been through something emotional in our lives that has taken its toll on our bodies. Whether it's illness, death of a family member, and, of course, divorce, few of us have escaped unscathed.

The great thing is that it's not too late to stop time from walking across your face! Most of the body's cells replace themselves frequently. You can dictate what kind of new cells replace the old cells by what you put into your body now. It's that simple. And it's not too late to start. Your choices today will dictate how you will look and feel tomorrow.

I want you to adopt a new philosophy for eating. I want it to become your default mode. It is based on clean, lean, unprocessed foods. You know, foods without a bar code!

It's this simple:

- Clean - meaning organic,
- Lean - meaning no animal fat, and
- Unprocessed foods - meaning not made by a company.
- Organic foods don't have antibiotics, growth hormones, pesticides, and added chemicals for preservation.

- The fat cells are where toxins are stored--in people and in animals. Our goal is to purge the toxins from our system, not to add more.
- Processed foods are, in most cases, anything premade and anything with a bar code. Anything you get from the inside aisles of the grocery store. Ready-to-eat, packaged anything. You get the idea. I'm not including the foods from the ready-to-eat cases in the higher end grocery stores.

This philosophy of eating may seem impossible when you have been relying on ready-made foods for convenience. But with a little planning, it's easy to accomplish. You just have to change your thinking. Raw veggies and fruits don't take any more work than cleaning, and they make great, tidy snacks that don't have to be refrigerated. Cooking different proteins at one time offers the convenience of having clean protein at the ready for quick meals and snacks. It's also cheaper than buying all that other stuff, having it stocked in your pantry, and it still requires labor to get it on the table.

With this philosophy you won't buy as much food at a time, because you want your food to be fresh. You will be amazed how easy grocery shopping becomes when you don't buy all those prepackaged foods.

Now for my soapbox . . . .

The Food Industry

Our goal here is to be healthy, vibrant, and youthful. Our goal is not to succumb to the many diseases and cancers that plague our generation. And, yes, I have a very strong opinion of how this has happened. Thanks to the industrialization of our food industry, the food produced now is over processed, disinfected, debugged, radiated, sprayed with toxins, chemically altered, artificially fertilized, and stripped of its original nutrients in the name of the almighty dollar. Not to mention the soil it comes from.

There are more unidentifiable ingredients in today's processed foods than ever before. And we wonder why the medical system is inundated with patients . . . . And then we have to channel billions of dollars into our medical industry to clean up the damage our food industry has caused. Where is the sense in that? Stop the insanity!

Our food industry fills its processed foods with sugar. The sugar makes the over-processed ingredients taste more palatable. Now I don't know if the food industry realizes that cancer cells feed on sugar or even if they care, but it sells the product. Again, for the almighty dollar. This cycle has to stop. If we just stop buying those processed foods and take better care of ourselves and our families, the industry will have to change. I know we have gotten used to the convenience factor, but this can be fixed. And I will show you how!

I've had too many things go wrong with my body over the years to leave my outcome to chance. And I don't want any more surgeries, especially if it's because I don't like the way I'm aging. I want to handle this in the least invasive, most effective way possible. I have many friends in my own world who have had breast cancer and colon cancer and three good friends who had thyroid cancer. Now that's just weird! That is too close to home. And they were all busy women who had careers and children and generally chose foods of convenience. Fast foods, processed foods, sweet foods--they thought they were making their life easier. They didn't realize that these choices were making their situations worse.

Our mothers probably did the same. The generation before ours got hit with the beginning of this processed craze. Remember when TV dinners hit the scene? Just the whole idea of getting to eat Mexican food, which was a treat, in a foil tray, sitting in front of the TV, was way cool. Our mothers fed us this faster, more convenient food, thinking it was fine because of the marketing of the product but having no idea what was in it. These products were too new to have any history to learn from.

The Diet of the Month

As an adult, I deal with a slow, unstable metabolism. I've had to accept the fact that I am what I am. Over the years, I have tried every hair-brained diet that has come along. I have lost, gained, lost, gained, lost, and yes, gained. Side note: The older you get, every time you lose weight after letting it sneak back onto your body, you have a chance of developing little "fat pockets" that don't go away and in the least expected places. You may think it's a tumor or something. You have your doctor check it out, and . . . it is a pocket of fat. It is harmless, but it's there, taunting you. Another good reason to take control of your weight and keep it there!

As an adolescent, I was a ballet dancer. I had to weigh in every week to make sure I wasn't getting too big. How's that for pressure on a teenager? I would starve myself, thinking it would make me lose weight, when really it was putting my body into a starvation mode. Then when I would actually eat again, my body would store the fuel into my fat cells in case I decided to starve myself again. Who knew? Obviously not me. And to this day, with all my roller-coaster dieting, I have just exacerbated the situation.

Like I said before, I live in the "Big Babe World." The only way I can maintain a happy balance in my life is to be as healthy as I can be. Nothing extreme, because as we all know by now, extreme never works, or lasts. But if I have a healthy philosophy of eating, I can maintain the size my body naturally defaults to. I can also better control the weight my body wants to invite to my "aging party." (That hurt to say!)

One thing I've learned over the years is you can fight Mother Nature all you want, but in the end, she wins. Genetics are huge. You are naturally predisposed to a certain body type. The sooner you make peace with this fact, the easier and more fun life will be. It's like styling your hair a certain way when your hair doesn't want to naturally do it. You work and work to achieve a certain style, but when you take a day off, or walk outside into the humidity, your hair goes back to the way it wants to be. Same with your body. You can diet and lose a lot of weight, but if you let up because it's too hard to maintain or you get busy with other things, your body goes back to the way it naturally wants to be.

Yes, there are those who swear that you can beat Mother Nature when it come to your body. But I think those people assume you have nothing else to do with your day than obsessively exercise and diet. I am personally busy enjoying my life and being the best I can be. I don't want to miss out on anything life has to offer because I'm looking at myself in a mirror, being totally preoccupied with how I look. Obsessing over one's appearance is never good!

If you adopt a healthy, clean, and lean eating philosophy, that will become your body's natural state. And then your mental energy is freed up to focus on other things, like new goals, reinventing yourself, enjoying life, or whatever is next on your "bucket list."

As for trying to be skinny, in all my years of reading and trying the "diet of the month," I realized that it was too hard to keep up with all the rules for "success." And I wasn't able to maintain those rules while feeding my family. Plus the rules kept changing! And if you bought some diet program's processed, pre-made meals, it would have cost more than my food budget for the month. Plus, having to buy processed foods to become healthier just doesn't make sense. Too many chemicals and additives are used in that stuff for the shelf life alone. That's what we are trying to get away from.

And as far as feeding your family is concerned, you are the cook, right? You dictate what is served in your house, no matter how much others complain. And more times than not, you are the one that buys the groceries. Even if you just add one or two healthy dishes at each meal and slowly change the way you prepare the protein, your kids will not even feel the transformation.

With my recipes, the dishes will taste hearty and yummy. The health factor is a side benefit for you and your kids. But you will know that the results you are achieving with this new philosophy of cooking and eating will affect their health for the rest of their lives. You are teaching them how to live healthy and make good choices. Who knows, it may also creep into other parts of their lives.

Inspirational Story:

A story that has inspired me is that of Christina Pirello. She is a whole foods cookbook writer and teacher. When she was diagnosed with leukemia as a young adult, it was already at the acute stage. She said she was just going to move to Italy and die. Then she met a man who turned her on to a macrobiotic diet. Having no other hope, she dove in headfirst. In two months, the doctors could tell a difference in her blood. In a year and a half, she had no more signs of leukemia in her blood at all and hasn't to this day. WOW! Now she cooks and preaches whole foods eating. She has cookbooks and a PBS cooking show, sharing the miracles of food.

Even Christina admits her way was extreme, but she had to gain control of her situation quickly. If you aren't suffering from a disease or illness yet, your approach can be more moderate. But why wait for that dreadful call from your doctor. Why not nip it in the bud, take control now, and reverse the signs of aging at the same time?

Cell Regeneration

Our body is designed to repair and heal itself. According to Stephanie Relfe, a kinesiologist, the type of nutrition we ingest dictates the type of replacement cells our body produces.

There are three ways in which a cell can replace itself:

1. a weaker cell due to poor nutrition, which is called degeneration;
2. the same strength of cell, which indicates no change, or a chronic condition; and

3. a stronger cell, due to vibrant, energetic raw materials fueling the body, which is called regeneration, or anti-aging.

According to the Newton BBS, operated by the Argonne National Laboratory, in conjunction with the U.S. Department of Energy, cells lining the inside and outside of our bodies divide every 20 or so hours: "So your skin cells, the lining of your intestines, and your blood cells are very actively living, dying and being replaced". Now that's what I want to hear! It's not too late to change your food choices and make a *big* difference in your future!

In this chapter, I will:

- give you a list of the vibrant, energetic raw materials for the "regeneration" of your cells through food choices,
- tell you how to choose produce and protein at the market,
- share a list of my favorite kitchen gadgets I think everyone should have,
- give you a list of foods and their peak seasons,
- discuss cooking techniques and beneficial food combinations,
- cover seasoning foods to enhance their natural flavors,
- list the physical benefits that many foods, herbs, and spices have on your body, and
- discuss how often you should eat and why.

How to Choose Produce and Protein

Fruits and Veggies

ALWAYS smell the fruit and vegetables wherever you shop. Most of the time the produce will taste the same as it smells. The stronger the smell, the stronger the taste. If it doesn't have much of a smell, it won't have much of a taste. You don't want too strong of a smell, though, because that might indicate overripeness. When you get used to the natural smells of produce, you will be a better judge of ripeness. Some produce doesn't have much smell, like celery, lettuce, avocados, potatoes, etc. With these types of produce, use a gentle touch or the skin color and skin surface to indicate freshness. For potatoes, there should be no green color of the skin, or "eyes".

The darker the color of the produce, the more antioxidants it will have. Whether it is the deep red of a red bell pepper, the rich orange color of a squash, the dark burgundy color of cherries, always choose the darkest colors of whatever your are buying. There is a fine line between perfect and overripeness. Choose wisely.

The stronger the onion smells, the more powerful the antioxidant benefit. When choosing garlic, make sure the cloves are large and tight, not dark, soft, or have sprouts coming out of the bulb. As for leeks, choose the ones that have as much white part as possible; you will get more for your money. The light green part is usable in recipes, but the dark green part is only good for stock. Red onions are milder and sweeter than white onions and very versatile. Onion progression in color and strength from strongest to weakest is white, yellow, red, yellow sweet, leeks, garlic, scallions, shallots and chives. These are all part of the allium family. Incredibly Healthy!

Tomatoes should be still attached to the vine, or stems, when possible. The stem tells you how fresh the tomato is. Also, tomatoes ripened on the vine have twice as much vitamin C as tomatoes grown in a hothouse. Good to know. Organic everything is always best, but when not available, buy the ones on the stem. Tomatoes should have that viney, green smell. If you don't know what I mean, smell one still with the stem. It should have a distinctive "live plant" type of aroma. When choosing cherry tomatoes, avoid shadows in the tomatoes. Those will be bitter. Also, your body absorbs 60% more lycopene from tomatoes when cooked in olive oil. Again, good to know. Also explore the heirloom varieties. They taste great and make a fun presentation.

Buy locally grown organic fresh herbs and everything else for that matter whenever possible. I recommend growing your own herbs in pots if you don't have suitable ground to use. The ground in my area is rocky, so most of my herbs are in pots.

Fruit is really important to smell before buying. Grapes, bananas, watermelons, and coconuts, of course, don't work; but most citrus and tropical fruits, strawberries, apples, pears, stone fruits, and some melons will taste the way they smell. And remember, the richer the color, the better for you.

Soapbox again: It is incredibly important to buy your produce from local farmers whenever possible. Local sources will only sell what is in season, so you will be getting only the freshest product. Local produce is often organic and won't have been gassed for "ripeness," because shipping isn't an issue. The produce is harvested usually the day it is brought to the farmers' market.

It's also important that we support our local agriculture. The food industry is now being run by a handful of conglomerates that don't have our health in mind. For them it's about the almighty dollar. This makes it increasingly difficult for local farmers to continue their quest for that all important connection with nature. If the local farmers don't strive to maintain that soon-to-be-lost art of man and land working in harmony, it will be gone forever. That will be another casualty of our industrialized existence.

Remember, when buying produce that is out of season, that produce has traveled thousands of miles to get to your store. It is coming from a part of the world where the growing season is completely different from yours. I'm talking about the other side of the world from you, which means it was picked before it was ripe so that it can withstand the trip. Then to get the produce to the color the consumer expects, it is "gassed" or artificially treated to bring it to its "ripened" state. The travel time also diminishes the health benefits the food had originally. The longer the produce is detached from the plant, the faster the vitamins, minerals, and antioxidants deteriorate, hence, the importance of buying locally when possible.

Fish

When choosing any seafood, ALWAYS smell it first. You can tell immediately if it is fresh. Seafood should smell like saltwater, not like fish. The fishier the smell, the older the product. And forget anything smelling like ammonia! Shellfish, like clams and mussels, should still be live. If the shells are closed, they are still living. If the shells are open but close by themselves when tapped on, they are still alive. If they don't close, they are dead and must be discarded. Same with cracked shells: discard immediately. Most clams, mussels, and oysters are now cultivated on strings, so they won't have as much, if any, grit in them as they used to.

When choosing a whole fish, make sure that the eyes are clear and fresh looking. No cloudiness or goop in the eyes. The gills need to be deep red and the scales, if still on, attached and uniform. These are signs of freshness.

When choosing fillets, smell is the most important indicator. Again, you want the fish to smell like saltwater, not like fish. Also, for salmon fillets or any more delicate fillets, the flesh should not be separating. This is a sign of deterioration. Usually, buying fish that has been previously frozen is preferable because most times the fish are flash frozen on the fishing boats or immediately upon cleaning. When fish has never been frozen, you want to be at the source. That way you know the fish is more likely to be fresh and not have traveled too far unfrozen.

For more unusual seafood, go to a fish market with a good reputation. Make sure the store sells their seafood inventory rapidly. You will be more likely to get the freshest product available in your area.

Meat

Look for a deep-red color for your beef choices. Again, smell. If it smells like meat, don't buy it. If the meat section smells like meat, don't buy from that store. Fresh meat smells fresh. Once you recognize the fresh meat smell, there will be no question. Older meat smells strong, while fresh meat smells faint. Don't buy brown meat, either. Oxidation turns meat brown, which indicates that the meat has been exposed to the air too long. Yes, aged beef is a darker reddish brown.

Only buy organic meat whenever possible. And grass-fed beef is always preferable. Cattle were not meant to eat grain; they were meant to eat grass. When cattle eat grain, especially corn, it causes them to become sick, hence the need for antibiotics. Now what about that is appetizing? Organic meat is free of those toxins and of genetically modified grain, which is what the industry feeds "nonorganic" beef. Also hormones, antibiotics and toxins are stored in the fat of the animal. Another reason for eating lean. Choose grass-fed, local, "natural" meat. The word "natural" has been badly abused by the food industry, so ask what that really means at your butcher's counter. Pick the leanest cuts you can find. Again, avoiding the toxins stored in the fat. If the animal eats it, you eat it!

Chicken should be organic and free-range. So should your eggs. Organic turkey is harder to find. Obviously, buy it when you can find it; otherwise, turkey is one of the leanest protein choices. Buy it in a store that has strict standards, such as Whole Foods. Ground, tenders, and breasts are all great choices. Even if it's not organic, it will be virtually free of fat and in turn freer of toxins.

Wild meats should follow the same requirements when possible. The fresher, the better. Also, the wilder the meat, the less contaminated by chemicals inadvertently ingested through the environment.

How to Choose Wines

I belong to the camp that thinks wine complements food and should be served with dinner. When choosing wine to accompany your meal, don't think color so much as flavor.

In general, the thicker the skin of the grape, the bigger the wine. The thinner the skin, the softer the wine. The warmer the climate the grapes are grown in, the warmer and bigger the wine. The cooler the climate, the lighter and fresher the wine. Lighter wines are usually more acidic. Darker wines are usually dryer and more tannic. Sweetness depends on the individual winemaker's style. Sparkling wines are great before the meal, with the first course and with desserts. OK, anytime really! The smaller the bubbles in the champagne or sparkling wine, the better the quality. Chenin Blanc, Sauvignon Blanc, Pinot Gris, and Rieslings are great with salads, vegetables, seafood, and shellfish. In general, these wines are also great with spicy foods. Chardonnay and Pinot Noir are great with light meats, poultry, light-colored sauces, pasta dishes with light sauce, seafood, and shellfish. Pinot Noir, Grenache, also known as Garnacha, and Tempranillo are great with pork, poultry dishes with heavier or darker sauces, and salmon. Cabernet Sauvignon, Grenache, Tempranillo, Malbec, Meritage and Syrah are great with red meats, wild mushrooms, Cognac sauces, and foods with attitude.

This just gives you a basic idea of what complements what. There is no way I can cover all the wine and food possibilities, but this gives you a basic guideline. But really, it all depends on your personal preferences. Drink what you like!

Explore the world of wine. You will learn that wine brings a celebration to everyday life!

Favorite Kitchen Gadgets

I try to avoid one-hit wonders in the kitchen. I want my gadgets to be multi functioning when possible. Too many gadgets require too much storage space. But some things you just gotta have.

Teakettle--electric, heats water almost instantly for any need--tea, hot water for a recipe--fabulous!

Indoor electric grill--cooks like a grill without having to brave the weather; not as much an essential as fun to have.

Microplane--can be used for nutmeg (always buy in seed form), cinnamon sticks, Parmesan and Romano cheeses (any hard cheese), garlic, the zesting of citrus fruits.

Whisks--multiple sizes, small for dressings, medium for everything else, and a large for fun.

Knife sharpener--handheld works fine, just use it on a cutting board at the edge of the counter (you don't want to cut the counter top by mistake); also once a year have your knives professionally sharpened. The cutting edge will last longer.

Oven thermometer--you never know when your oven will go on the blink (I hate that!). Plus, ovens can have a 25 - 50 degree differential.

Cutting boards--again, multiple sizes; small for lemons and limes, medium for small jobs, large for big jobs; also have at least one plastic or synthetic board specifically for raw meat, poultry, and fish that can preferably fit in the dishwasher. You don't want to contaminate wooden boards with raw protein.

Salad servers--I love to collect interesting ones.

Coffee grinders--large one for coffee (ground fresh every morning) and small one for dried spices; don't mix the two!

Spice grinder--comes with four individual glass jars with lids and has a grinder attachment that fits on the top of the jars; grinds dried herbs when needed, refreshing the oils of the dried herbs; found at Williams Sonoma.

Emersion blender--fabulous way to puree hot mixtures without having to do it in batches in a processor or blender, especially if you just want to thicken something for texture without pureeing the whole batch.

Sorbet maker--really easy way to make a last-minute, healthy dessert that everyone will love.

Knives--a good set of kitchen knives is mandatory! Splurge once and you are covered forever. You can get them in a set, which is cheaper, or buy individual knives if you already have some good ones to supplement.

- I really like the Santoku knife. It can easily take the place of a chef's knife. The blade is a little thinner than a chef's knife, which means it needs a different sharpener for the home.

- A bread knife is good to have, because it can be used for anything you would need a serrated edge for, like tomatoes, bread, pastries, roasted meats, etc.
- A paring knife is also important. I like the four inch paring knife best, but get whatever feels the most comfortable in your hand. You will have more control, which is key!
- It's important to take good care of your knives. Hand wash them. Period. Dishwasher detergent will dull the blade's edge. Also, immediately rinse knives that have been used to cut anything acidic, like onions or citrus fruits. The acidity will corrode the blade's edge.

Handheld citrus juicer/squeezer--you can put half a lemon or lime in the bowl and squeeze the juice out, leaving the seeds in the bowl of the squeezer.

Garlic press--crushes the garlic, leaving the skin in the press.

Vegetable brush--gentle; great for cleaning fresh corn on the cob and mushrooms.

Vegetable scrubber--in glove form, or firmer brush; great for carrots and potatoes so you don't have to peel them, since most of the nutrients reside in or just below the skins.

Vegetable peeler--you need a heavy-duty one that can tackle cucumbers as well as butternut squash.

Salad spinner--worth the storage space; gets the water off lettuce leaves and fresh herbs, so the excess water won't dilute your dressing.

Tongs--couldn't cook without them; a long and short set; multiple uses from turning food while cooking, to tossing salad, to cooking food on a grill.

Outdoor grilling tools--metal spatulas with long handles, one regular sized flat surface and one with a long flat surface for fish; tongs with long handles; skewers with heat-proof handles for kabobs; and, of course, a metal brush to clean off the grates between grilling.

Meat thermometer--to cook protein to perfection; for checking internal temperature.

Salt & pepper mills--a good set of salt and pepper grinders in case you want to use coarse sea salt, and the nonnegotiable fresh peppercorns.

Measuring spoons and cups--at least one good set of each that is dishwasher safe; as for the cups, get a set for measuring liquids and a set for measuring dry ingredients.

Pastry scraper--truly helps get sticky dough off the cutting board and makes picking up chopped foods easy.

Corkscrew--my favorite is a waiter's corkscrew; it's the easiest to use.

Bamboo steamer--if you get one with multiple baskets, you can steam more than one item at a time; keeps the nutrients in the food.

Seasons for Food

Look for abundant bins and falling prices in your grocery store, usually indicating the produce that is in season. This will be the time of the year when the produce is at its peak in flavor and nutritional benefits.

Shop as often as possible at your local farmers' market. The food is usually fresher, and you are supporting the local farmer. Again, support the organic farmer when possible.

Spring

- asparagus
- artichokes
- beets
- broccoli
- cabbage family
- carrots
- collard greens
- fava beans
- variety of greens
- herbs
- lettuce
- new potatoes (May)
- peas
- snow peas (May)
- spinach (May)
- sprouts and tendrils

- strawberries
- tangelos

Summer

- apples
- asparagus
- basil
- beets
- beans
- bell peppers
- blackberries
- blueberries
- cabbage family
- cantaloupe
- carrots
- cauliflower
- casaba melon
- cherries
- corn
- cucumbers
- eggplant
- English or field peas
- grapes
- garlic
- herbs
- honeydew melon
- variety of hot peppers
- kale
- leeks
- lettuce
- lima beans
- variety of melons
- mushrooms
- nectarines
- okra
- onions
- peaches
- plums
- potatoes

- raspberries
- snow peas
- strawberries (early)
- sugar peas
- spinach
- squash
- stone fruits
- tomatoes
- watermelon

Fall

- apples
- asparagus
- bell peppers
- blackberries
- broccoli
- butternut or any winter squash
- cabbage family
- Chinese cabbage
- cantaloupe (through Sept.)
- cranberries
- cucumbers (Sept.)
- eggplant (Sept.)
- English or field peas
- fennel
- garlic
- variety of greens
- grapes
- herbs
- variety of hot peppers
- kale
- lima beans
- mushrooms
- nuts
- okra
- pears
- pecans
- persimmons
- pomegranates

- pumpkin
- white and sweet potatoes
- quince
- raspberries
- rutabagas
- sweet corn
- swiss chard
- tomatoes
- turnips
- watermelons

Winter

- apples
- broccoli
- brussels sprouts
- cauliflower
- citrus fruits
- eggplant
- figs
- pears
- grapefruit
- herbs
- variety of lettuces
- mushrooms
- oranges
- pecans
- pumpkin
- white and sweet potatoes
- squash
- tangerines

There is no way I can list all the fruits and vegetables, but this list gives you a good idea of the growing seasons for the most popular choices.

Again, look for the overflowing bins and good prices for your indication of what is in season.

A lot of varieties of fruits and vegetables are available year-round. But read the labels. If the produce is from the other side of the world, it has been off the plant or out of the ground for a long time. It had to have been picked prematurely and possibly gassed for travel endurance and shelf life. By the time it reaches you, the nutritional benefits are minimal.

Cooking Techniques

Good to Know

Always start your recipes with the best ingredients that you can afford. The success of cooking depends on the freshness of your ingredients.

Your goal is to eat as many different colors of natural foods at every meal as possible. This means consciously including a variety of colors when you plan and when you shop. Salads help here. Also keep your dressings simple, no creamy versions. The same consideration is needed for ordering off a menu at a restaurant. Make sure you choose wisely. Also, get the dressings on the side. Your health is at stake!

When buying dried herbs, get them from a bulk section of a grocery store that has a high turnover rate of its inventory. The cost of bulk herbs is minimal compared to buying them in the spice aisle in bottles, which shoots up the cost. Reuse old bottles if that's how you like to store your spices, but keeping them in small plastic zipped bags, in a dark, cool cabinet is just fine. The cost is fractional and less storage area is required. Just make sure you label what is in each bag. Also, don't buy large amounts of herbs at a time unless you have a specific need for a recipe. You want to use your herbs within a couple of months. Age diminishes the dried herbs' original flavor and health benefits. You will want to refresh your supply at least every season, so don't buy too much at a time.

When cooking with dried herbs, either rub them in your hands first or use an herb grinder. This releases the natural oils and flavors in the herbs. You can also add dried herbs in the browning stage of cooking a protein. The herbs will get toasted, permeating the protein and adding a new dimension of flavor to the dish.

When buying beans, dried is fine, but canned beans are one of the few vegetables that is comparable to the dried or fresh versions. Also, when cooking beans, don't add salt to the pot until the beans are almost done. The salt prevents the beans from softening.

When buying ground turkey, always get the leanest percentage you can find. Also, get organic whenever possible, or buy from a store with rigid quality standards. Remember, the cleaner the protein, the better for your body. When browning the ground turkey, cook it in one to two tablespoons olive oil for "good fat" over medium heat for ease of cooking.

Also add your chopped onion and salt and pepper when browning to give the meat a deeper level of flavor and moisture. Adding your herbs while browning will also give the final turkey flavor another interesting dimension, along with more antioxidants.

When cooking breakfast, try sautéing chopped onions in 1 tablespoon olive oil, add tomatoes, spinach or arugula and 2 beaten eggs with salt and pepper to taste. Cook to your desired consistency, and breakfast is served. Look at all the nutritional benefits you've put into one simple meal! Eggs are good for your eyes, heart, liver, and brain. By adding the spinach, tomatoes, and onions, you are also benefiting your circulation, lungs, stomach, blood pressure, and on and on. And that was just breakfast!

There are so many simple things you can do to make your food intake more beneficial to your health. Adding a squeeze of fresh lemon juice and a sprinkle of cinnamon to a fresh fruit salad adds great flavor and extra antioxidants, making it a fabulously delicious and healthy treat. Also, the more hot pepper and cayenne you can add to your daily diet, the higher your metabolism and better your circulation will be. The more herbs and spices you use in your cooking, the more antioxidant benefits you will achieve.

Another good rule of thumb is to not peel your carrots or white and red potatoes. Get a vegetable scrubber that is effective, and scrub the dirt off the skins. The skins add flavor, texture, nutrients, and fiber. Just get use to it. The benefits far outweigh the adjustment.

Add a cinnamon stick or cinnamon chips to your hot tea. Add organic cocoa powder to your coffee. Both will increase your antioxidant benefits and add to your flavor profile.

Choose raw organic sugar over white refined sugar. The less processed, the better. Same with salt. Choose sea salt over white refined salt. Refined salt and sugar are stripped of their natural nutrients. Extreme refinement also adds chemicals that we are trying to avoid. Keep it as clean and natural as possible. Another sweetener option is agave nectar. It is sweeter than sugar and is lower on the glycemic index.

When making family favorites that contain ground beef, try substituting ground turkey for a healthy alternative. There are many ways to give ground turkey depth of flavor, so that no one misses the beef flavor. You can also get your family used to not having that "beef" flavor as their familiar protein source. And don't forget, you can always use organic beef broth in turkey dishes for that "beef" flavor. Chili, spaghetti with meat sauce, homemade pizza, and even hamburgers can be made with ground turkey and taste great. Explore available turkey products now offered in grocery stores and see which ones you like best. I'm providing you some recipes in the back of the book to give you ideas of herbs and spices that can add depth of flavor to your dishes made with turkey.

If you do choose ground beef, make sure that it is grass-fed, organic, and as lean as possible. Remember, any toxins are stored in the fat. So avoid the fat. Grass-fed beef has more omega-3 and other important nutrients than corn-fed beef has. Plus, cows were not genetically made to process grain; they are supposed to eat grass. So with grass-fed beef, you don't get all the side effects in the meat that comes from cows that are forced to eat food that is unnatural for their species.

Since pasta is a staple in many households, buy the whole grain varieties. Also, choose brown rice over any white rice. Get used to the taste. Whole grains and brown rice have a nuttier flavor than their white counterparts have. Just don't eat "white" anymore.

Another great grain option is quinoa, which is not a grain at all. It is the seed of the chenopodium plant. It is actually related to spinach, beets and Swiss chard. Quinoa is high in protein, calcium, iron and a variety of vitamins and amino acids. It tastes nutty and yummy. You should try it. Quinoa can be used in place of rice and is much better for you.

This is a tip for making a salad ahead of time: make your dressing in a large bowl, then add your ingredients, with the salad greens on the top, and cover until ready to use. Just before serving, toss the salad, making sure the dressing gets stirred up to coat all the ingredients. This gives you the flexibility of making the salad before your guests arrive, without the greens wilting from prolonged contact with the dressing.

Add fresh-squeezed lime juice at the end of making chicken soup to perk up the flavor. Lemon juice can add a spark to steamed vegetables, like broccoli, artichokes, and spinach. Lemon juice also brings seafood to life, sprinkled over fish fillets, shrimp, and shellfish. Fabulous!

When you are making a cocktail, always use fresh-squeezed juices.

When using fresh herbs in a dish, add them at the end of the cooking process. That will keep the fresh flavor of the herbs intact. Cooking fresh herbs too long mutes the fresh taste that you are looking for.

An old Italian kitchen tip: when storing potatoes, put an apple in the basket or bag used for storage. The apple will keep the potatoes from developing the "eyes."

And don't forget the cheese. When using cheese, especially for cooking, choose the more aged versions, like aged provolone, Parmesan, and extra sharp cheddar. The more aged the cheese, the more flavor it will have, which means that you can use less with more flavor. This is a great tip if you are concerned about calories but still want flavor. Also, avoid using cheeses that are unnaturally colored, like yellow/orange cheddar. Additives give the cheese its color, and we don't want those chemicals in our diet.

When "roasting" anything, a good rule of thumb is a 400-degree oven. When "toasting" nuts or anything else, a 350-degree oven is safe. Since most ovens have a 50-degree heat differential, you have that much play in temperature when cooking in an oven. If you are cooking one dish at 350 and another dish at 400, you can usually cook them both at 375 and adjust the time for the temperature difference of each dish. This does not apply for baking, where you have to be much more precise.

When measuring anything syrupy or sticky, spray the measuring spoon or cup with vegetable spray first, and all of the ingredient will easily slide out of the utensil for a perfect measure.

Now for salt: I prefer sea salt because table salt has been so stripped of every natural flavor and nutrient. And in that stripping process, chemicals are added, which we don't want in our food or bodies. Sea salt has a subtle, soft flavor that naturally enhances the flavor of everything. You use less sea salt than table salt when seasoning your food. You will need to season to taste when you first start using sea salt, because again, it takes less sea salt than the old table salt. Another interesting tidbit, if you normally use kosher salt, or it is called for in a recipe and you want to switch to sea salt instead, use half the amount of sea salt as you would kosher salt. Kosher salt has larger pieces than a finer sea salt has, so you need half as much of the sea salt. Don't forget to taste.

More about salt: A restaurant trick is to add a little salt at each stage of preparing a dish, never all at once. This will bring out the most flavor in each stage, giving you a greater depth of flavor. For example, when cooking soup, add a little salt when you are sautéing the onions and garlic, then add a little more after you add your vegetables, and finally add more after you pour in the stock, bringing the total amount of salt to equal the original amount called for in the recipe. After the recommended cooking time, taste for seasoning and adjust if necessary. If you add the salt all at once, your dish will have a "shallow" taste. If you add it in stages, your dish will have more depth of flavor.

Substitutions

- Substitute tzatziki sauce for ranch dip or dressing. The kids will love it just as much, and they will have the added benefits of the yogurt, cucumbers, and herbs.
- Substitute 2% Greek-style yogurt for sour cream. You can't tell the difference, no lactose issues, and added probiotic benefits.
- Substitute your favorite dip with one made from 2% Greek yogurt. Make it yourself with a flavor packet that you would add to sour cream.
- Substitute lemon for vinegar in vinaigrettes or at least half and half.
- Use coconut oil in the place of olive oil when that interesting flavor of coconut will work with the dish; coconut oil has been shown to contribute to weight loss and lowers cholesterol.

Time-savers

Something I find helpful is to have cooked and seasoned (salt and peppered) meat in the refrigerator for easy access. Cooked ground beef or turkey that is ready to use can make soft tacos, chili, lettuce wraps, nachos, pizza, etc., quickly and easily. Cooked chicken breasts can be made into pizza, stir-fry, wraps, and the afore mentioned in very little time. If you always have a lean protein available, you will be more likely to eat something good for you when in a hurry. And protein intake is important for muscle building and maintenance.

Adding dried thyme when browning ground beef or dried oregano to ground turkey will give an additional layer of flavor to the meat. Also, get one of those dried herb grinders. They are great. They reignite the oils in the dried herbs, making them more aromatic and flavorful in a smaller, more digestible size. And don't forget, the more herbs and spices you add to your food, the more nutritional benefits you will add to your diet.

Take a little time to prepare vegetables in snack sizes. Store in a zipped bag in the refrigerator for easy access. You will be more likely to grab veggies as a snack when they are readily accessible. This also saves time when cooking dishes that call for veggies. These are already halfway prepped for you. Mix some Greek yogurt with your favorite dip mix or my creole seasoning, and you will always have a yummy snack that is also nutritious.

Get a one-tablespoon measured topper for your oil bottles, you know, olive oil, grape seed oil, whatever you use. I get decorative 750 ml. bottles from a craft store and the topper from The Container Store. It's pretty, and I always know how much oil I am using without additional utensils. Make sure you store your oils away from light and heat. A pantry is perfect, but not on the counter.

Since we want to add fresh garlic to as many dishes as possible for the flavor and health benefits, take time to chop a head of garlic and store it in a glass jar. Cover the garlic completely with extra virgin olive oil and store it in the refrigerator. This way you have garlic prepped and at the ready. Use it. A garlic press is also handy for making garlic more user-friendly.

Combinations

There are certain foods that are more readily absorbed by the body if ingested with other ingredients. My cookbook, **Eating on Purpose**, will cover this in more detail. Here are a few:

- Cabbage--cabbage can be hard to digest, but cancer hates it! So we are going to do what it takes to make it easily absorbed. Cumin seed helps aid in digestion and adds a great complementing flavor; also sauerkraut is very good for your digestive system.
- Carrots--the carotenoids need fat to be absorbed; eat raw carrots with dip or dressing (with some fat in it); sautéing carrots with olive oil or a little organic butter and adding fresh dill at the end; roasting carrots, brussels sprouts, sweet potatoes, and onions tossed in extra-virgin olive oil, dried thyme, salt and pepper, and cooked on a baking sheet in a 425-degree oven for 30 minutes--divine!
- Spinach--the lutein in spinach needs fat to be absorbable; spinach eaten with eggs gives you a double dose of lutein because the fat in the egg makes the lutein in both more absorbable; the iron in spinach is better absorbed with vitamin C; sautéing spinach in olive oil and garlic is fabulous, with a little chopped red bell pepper or tomato and a grating of Parmesan cheese; try spinach salads with hard-boiled eggs, dried cranberries, a sprinkle of feta and chopped almonds, and olive oil in the dressing; variations of spinach salad with strawberries or mandarin oranges are also fabulous.

- Tomatoes--the carotenoids are better absorbed when eaten with some fat, like avocados, olive oil, eggs, nuts; tomato's main carotenoid is lycopene; cooked forms of tomatoes are also highly beneficial in avoiding prostate cancer; use tomatoes and avocados in salads, with chopped almonds in an olive oil vinaigrette; prepare dishes with tomato sauces or tomato products that have been cooked.

Tasty Compliments

The flavors of some foods are naturally enhanced by other foods. Some fabulous combinations:

- Mangos and cinnamon have an affinity for each other.
- Most variations of fruit salad are fabulous with cinnamon, as are berries, apples, pears, pineapple and bananas.
- Nutmeg enhances spinach, dark leafy greens, sweet potatoes, cream dishes, cheese sauces, egg dishes, oatmeal, and acorn and butternut squash.
- Citrus juice complements a multitude of foods, whether it is lemon or lime; fruit salads, green salads, seafoods, chicken soup, tea, bubble water, flat water, tuna fish salad, broccoli, artichokes, eggplant, tomato and cucumber salad, you name it--experiment!
- Eggplant, tomatoes, and lemon are great together.
- Rosemary is great with poultry, pork, lamb, chicken soup, white potatoes, vegetable soup, and mushrooms.
- Thyme enhances red meats, poultry, pork, seafood, roasted vegetables, mushrooms; is good in combination with rosemary and bay leaf; adds a deep European flavor to veggies.
- Bay leaf is fabulous with beef, beef-based dishes, hearty vegetable soup, and mushrooms.
- Oregano complements any tomato-based dish, pork, poultry, salads, and vinaigrettes.
- Marjoram is milder than oregano but a similar flavor profile and can be used in the same way.
- Sage loves turkey, bread dressings, black-eyed peas, lentils, and squash.
- Basil sings in tomato dishes, be it salads, tomato sauces, soups; also is great in pesto sauce; combine tomato, fresh mozzarella,

and basil with a drizzle of extra virgin olive oil and sea salt; try garlic, onions, lemon, and extra-virgin olive oil; when cooking with fresh basil, add at the end of the cooking process to preserve the food's bright flavor.
- Mint complements peas, Asian dishes, middle-eastern dishes, fruit salads, fruit desserts, tea, yogurt, and yogurt dishes.
- Paprika is used to enhance goulashes, stews, chicken dishes, and paella and adds a smokiness to vegetable soup; is also used as a garnish for color and adds a slight smoky flavor; is good sprinkled on garlic bread.
- Walnuts and morel mushrooms have an affinity for each other, as do walnuts and cream with nutmeg.
- Beets and orange juice and beets and pears complement each other (fresh of each are best).
- Carrots and cumin have an affinity for each other, as do carrots and dill.
- Lime juice and fresh tuna are fabulous together.

Again, there are too many fabulous flavor combinations to list here. These are just the most common complements.

Nutritional Benefits

Food is nature's medicine. If you eat with this in mind, you will make better food choices and be healthier for it.

The following lists provide you with nutritional benefits of some of the more commonly used vegetables, fruits, herbs, and spices. You will be amazed at the power of food.

These foods will benefit your current and future health, but are not intended to replace medications you may be taking for any pre-existing conditions.

VEGETABLES

- artichokes--liver cleansing; helps digestion; helps protect against cardiovascular disease; promotes eye health
- arugula--bone building; promotes eye health; cancer fighting; diuretic; digestive aid; supports liver health
- asparagus--blood cleansing; bone building; cancer fighting; anti-inflammatory, antioxidant; strengthens blood vessels; diuretic

- beans--lowers risk of cancer, heart disease, diabetes, and obesity; lowers cholesterol; helps regulate blood sugar and insulin; inhibits cancer cell reproduction and growth of tumors
- beets--blood and liver cleansing; cancer fighting
- broccoli--cancer and tumor fighting; antioxidant; detoxifier; helps promote eye health; helps protect against macular degeneration
- brussels sprouts--cancer fighting; bone building
- cabbage--and anything from the Brassica family, like broccoli, brussels sprouts, cauliflower, collard greens, kale, any type or color of cabbage--incredibly cancer fighting; blood and liver cleansing; increases ratio of "good" estrogen metabolites to the "bad" ones; helps protect against pesticides and other toxins; antioxidant, anti-inflammatory; helps protect against cardiovascular disease; promotes eye health
- carrots--antioxidants; helps protect against bladder, cervical, prostate, colon, larynx, esophageal, and postmenopausal breast cancer; inhibits tumor growth; protects eyes, helps prevent macular degeneration and cataracts; immune system stimulator
- celery--helps control appetite; stems carb cravings; aids in digestion; lowers blood pressure; increases blood flow; lowers stress levels; helps renew joints, bones, arteries, and all connective tissue; inhibits tumor growth
- dandelion greens--one of the most nutrient-rich vegetables; detoxifies the liver; aids in digestion, heartburn, and constipation; natural diuretic; great for reducing water retention from PMS and edema in lower legs and ankles; reduces blood pressure; helps promote eye health and protects against macular degeneration; antioxidant
- eggplant--powerful antioxidant; helps protect against free-radical damage to your cells and DNA (which contributes to aging); helps protect against oxidative damage to brain tissue
- fennel--beneficial in stopping stomach cramps, gas, and aids digestion; anti-inflammatory; cleansing properties; diuretic
- garlic--antioxidant, antiviral, antimicrobial, antiparasitic, antibacterial; lowers bad cholesterol without lowering the

good; helps reduce plaque in arteries; helps prevent platelets in blood from sticking together; cancer fighting; helps prevent common cold

- green beans--also French, runner, snap, wax, Italian beans; good folate source, which prevents neural tube defects in babies; helps prevent heart disease, stroke, dementia, and peripheral vascular disease
- horseradish--cancer fighting; inhibits tumor growth and suppresses growth of existing tumors; helps liver detoxify carcinogens; actually better for you when processed
- lentils--don't produce as much gas as other legumes; helps control cholesterol and blood sugar; lowers risk of heart disease and cancer
- onions--cancer fighting; protects against prostate and esophageal cancer; builds strong bones; antioxidant, anti-inflammatory, antibiotic, antiviral; helps protect against cancer and heart disease; relieves asthma and hay fever symptoms; lowers blood pressure
- spinach--bone building; cancer fighting; reduces inflammation; retards age-related declines in brain function; protects against eye disease and vision loss; brain food; mood and feeling enhancer; lowers triglycerides; helps reduce plaque formation; supports memory; natural appetite suppressant
- split peas-- promotes bone health; good source of fiber
- sweet potatoes--high in fiber; cancer fighting properties; antioxidant, anti-inflammatory
- tomatoes--cancer fighting; helps reduce blood pressure; reduces risk of heart attacks; helps prevent atherosclerosis; disease fighting; helps prevents macular degeneration

FRUITS

- apples--benefits your liver and muscles; aids in digestion; controls cholesterol and blood sugar
- avocados--antioxidant; lowers cholesterol; protects the prostate; reduces risk of cancer and diabetes; protects against heart disease; promotes eye and skin health
- apricots--need to be eaten with some fat for maximum absorption of the betacarotene; strong antioxidant; reduce risk

of lung and colon cancers; helps protect against arthritis; more health benefits from the fresh fruit than from dried version

- blueberries--ultimate memory food; guards against mental deterioration, loss of coordination and balance; antioxidant, anti-inflammatory; helps neurons talk to each other and promotes new neuron growth; promotes urinary health; lowers blood pressure; helps prevent macular degeneration; promotes cardiovascular health; inhibits cancer cell production
- cantaloupe--appetite control; lowers risks of heart disease and stroke; lowers blood pressure; immune system booster; increases resistance to infections; promotes eye health; bone builder
- cherries--anti-inflammatory, anti-aging, anticancer, antiviral, antibacterial; inhibits tumor growth
- cranberries--stimulates circulation; prevents and treats urinary tract infections; improves complexion; aids in digestion; astringent properties; very powerful antioxidants; inhibits food-related pathogen growth; inhibits cancer cell growth; reduces plaque on teeth; helps prevent stomach ulcers
- figs--great for fiber; helps control blood sugar; source of calcium and potassium; lowers blood pressure and risks of stroke
- grapes--reduces risk of cardiovascular disease and cancer; antimutagen, anti-aging, anti-inflammatory, powerful antioxidants; helps protect cells from DNA-damaging free radicals; natural antihistamine
- kiwi--cancer fighting; helps prevent heart disease; reduces oxidative stress or cellular damage to DNA and repairs damage that has occurred; blood thinner; helps protect against asthma
- lemon and lemon juice---cancer fighting; antioxidants, anti-inflammatory
- papaya--natural digestive enzymes; anti-inflammatory, antioxidant; promotes eye health; reduces risk of lung and colon cancer; reduces risk of rheumatoid arthritis
- strawberries--inhibits tumor initiation; helps protect against cervical, breast, and liver cancer; helps protect brain and memory; inhibits growth of tumors caused by certain carcinogens

HERBS AND SPICES

- basil--soothes pain; nausea treatment; helps relieve nervous stress; soothes headaches; antiseptic; stomach tonic
- cayenne--helps retard coughs and colds; promotes eye health; enhances circulation and metabolism; aids in digestion; kills bacteria; beneficial effects on insulin levels
- cinnamon--powerful antioxidant; protects against stomach ulcers; helps regulate blood sugar; antimicrobial, anti-inflammatory; benefits digestion; relieves nausea; lowers triglycerides and cholesterol; helps reduce blood pressure
- ginger--soothes upset stomachs; helps prevent nausea and vomiting; helps prevent seasickness; helps prevent morning sickness; antioxidant, anti-inflammatory, antimicrobial, antiviral; good for soothing arthritic pain; boosts immune system; improves circulation; good blood thinner
- oregano--the herb with the highest antioxidant activity; antifungal, antibacterial, antiparasitic, antimutagenic, anticarcinogenic properties, and anti-inflammatory; digestive aid; supports joint function
- parsley--aids detoxification; inhibits tumors; antibacterial, anti-inflammatory; cancer fighting; eye protecting; bone building; benefits kidneys and tissue renewal
- rosemary--antioxidant, antibiotic, antiviral and anti-inflammatory properties; helps protect against asthma, liver disease, and heart disease; inhibits cancer and tumors; promotes memory and brain function
- sage--antimicrobial, antiviral, antioxidant and anti-inflammatory properties; helps lower blood pressure; memory enhancer; combats indigestion, excessive perspiration, and sore throats; helps reduce menopausal night sweats
- thyme--powerful antiseptic, antioxidant, and anti-inflammatory; aids in digestion; relieves chest and respiratory problems

In the Appendix II are the nutritional benefits in chart form to aid in comprehension.

These lists are just some of the commonly used vegetables, fruits, herbs, and spices used in most households. I will have a more complete listing in my upcoming cookbook, ***Eating on Purpose***.

How Often to Eat and Why

We've been raised to believe that eating three big meals a day is sufficient. Any more is gluttony. That idea was fine when we did manual labor every day. Obviously, that isn't relevant anymore. We live in a cerebral world now. We have to rethink the fueling of our body.

Today's lifestyle is more sedentary, shall we say. More of us are sitting at a desk eight hours a day, not moving more than to go down the hall occasionally. Then when we get home, we are busy trying to take care of all the other requirements that make our daily existence work. If you don't have kids at home anymore, there isn't quite as much to do around the house, but we still have our own list of chores. And if the kids are still there . . . well, you know what that means. Chaos!

The message here is that you have ups and downs in any given day. The three-times-a-day meal plan does not benefit your lifestyle anymore.

Now you need a constant energy level to be as productive and vibrant as possible. Now is when your body will benefit from more frequent, smaller meals in a day.

Every time you eat, your blood sugar elevates. How high it goes depends on what and how much you eat. If you eat a lot, it goes high; if you eat less, the lower that high will be. Lower is our goal. We don't want spikes.

The idea here is that your body can use the calories ingested in a more steady and efficient manner if they come in smaller quantities, more often. The result is a steadier blood sugar level and a more balanced metabolism. This also eliminates the highs and lows you get from the old "three-meal-a-day" plan.

When you eat three times a day, you tend to eat more at each meal. Then when your body is processing the food, it has to find places for the energy to go. If you are sitting back down to your desk or going to sleep, your body just stores that unused energy into fat deposits, ideally for future use. (Yeah, right!) If you eat and then actually do something physical, the energy will be used by the muscles to support that activity.

The smaller the amounts of food you eat each time, the more stable your metabolism will stay. The more level your blood sugar will stay. The more consistent your energy level will stay. The fewer highs and lows you will have because of food. This gives you a steadier energy stream and a clearer, sharper mind.

This type of eating also contributes to maintaining a healthy weight. You keep a constant metabolic level and that prevents fat storage. Hooray!

It also gives you the energy needed to be as vibrant and vivacious as you want to be. Again, hooray!

I've listed below an example of a typical day of meals. You want to strive for eating five small meals per day.

Your first meal should be no later than 30 minutes after you wake up. Your last meal should not be past 7:00 p.m. when possible.

Your meals should be in three-hour intervals. This will keep your metabolism at a steady level.

The following example is a good guide when you are trying to keep excess fat off. And, when a celebration comes along, enjoy yourself. That's why we strive to eat like this the rest of the time, so we can splurge on festive occasions!

Typical breakfast:

- 2 ounces of protein, like eggs, salmon, tofu, low-fat yogurt
- 1 cup fruit, like grapefruit, peaches, plums, cherries, pineapple, berries, cantaloupe, honeydew, apples, pears

Typical mid-morning snack:

- 2 ounces of protein, like eggs, salmon, tuna, tofu
- 1 cup fruit, like grapefruit, peaches, plums, cherries, pineapple, berries, cantaloupe, honeydew, apples, pears

Typical lunch:

- 2 ounces of protein, like chicken breast, turkey breast, tuna, salmon, lean pork, tofu, shrimp, crab, scallops
- 1/2 cup complex carbohydrate, like brown rice, sweet potato, squash, barley, oatmeal, quinoa
- 1 cup veggies, like mixed salad, green beans, carrots, and celery, just about any other vegetable

Typical mid-afternoon snack:

- 2 ounces of protein, like almonds, walnuts, tuna, chicken breast, turkey breast, salmon
- 1 cup veggies, like carrot and celery sticks with 2% Greek yogurt dip, salad, whatever veggies you love

Typical dinner:

- 3 ounces of protein, like salmon, tuna, chicken breast, turkey breast, lean pork, shrimp, scallops, lobster, crab, fish, lean red meat

- 1/2 cup complex carbohydrate, like brown rice, barley, sweet potato, squash, turnips, quinoa, whole wheat pasta
- 1 cup veggies, just about any of them

Your goal is to spread your protein intake over the day, not to eat it all at once. That's why it is listed in small amounts each time. This is to promote muscle maintenance and development. If you eat red meat, eat less per portion and stick with the leanest cuts, like tenderloin, sirloin, eye of round, and the leanest ground beef. Buy only grass-fed beef. Otherwise, choose a different protein. Make your pork choices the leanest cuts possible.

Nuts are another good choice for protein. Just be aware of the fat and calorie content that nuts have. Almonds and walnuts have good fat, but the calories still add up quickly. About 22-25 nuts is a good serving.

As you will notice, I don't have much dairy listed as a protein option. I like low-fat yogurt for the probiotic benefits, but other than that, it's too hard to stay in control with dairy. And some of us have lactose issues. Cheese should be used as a treat or flavor accent; otherwise, calcium can be acquired through other means, like broccoli, supplements, etc. And when using cheese in cooking, use an aged version when possible. You get more flavor with less quantity.

Fruit is fine, as long as it is in its natural state. Most fruit juices have high sugar content, and the fiber benefit has been removed. It is easier to regulate the amount of sugar you ingest if it's in its full fruit form. Also, eat your fruit earlier in the day. You have a better chance of burning off the sugars from the fruit if eaten by your lunch meal. But when given the choice of fruit or a "sweet" for dessert, choose the fruit. Natural sugar is always better than artificial or added.

Unless you are predisposed to diabetes or have already been diagnosed as having diabetes, you should be fine eating moderate amounts of fruit. Just don't get carried away. Our goal is the health benefit fruit provides, while keeping your blood sugar at a stable level, not shot to the moon. If you are diabetic, your doctor will tell you what you can eat, not me.

Cut out all white, simple carbs if possible. If it's not possible, cut way down. An occasional potato is OK because it is natural. But it turns to sugar immediately in your system, shooting up your blood sugar, so don't eat potatoes often. Choose only whole grain pasta if you must have pasta. And nix the white rice. Brown rice has a nuttier flavor anyway. Don't forget quinoa as a good substitute for white rice and as a good source of protein.

As far as veggies are concerned, you can eat pretty much whatever you want, whenever you want. Just keep them clean and lean in their preparation. And always choose organic when possible.

Another important goal is to eat as many "colors" as possible each and every day. Every color in the fruit and vegetable world offers vital nutrients and health benefits to your body naturally. And remember, the darker and richer the color, the more nutrients contained in the food. So try to have as many different colors on your plate at each meal as possible.

With a clean, lean, natural food goal, there is no room for processed foods. There are too many hidden ingredients in processed foods. Not everything is listed on the labels, and chances are you don't recognize half the ingredients that *are* listed. Too many preservatives, sugars, salts from nonorganic sources, not to mention chemical preservatives. In my upcoming cookbook, ***Eating on Purpose***, I will give you fast, easy recipes for making meals fabulous AND healthy.

If this way of eating seems strict to you, there is good news. You get one day off a week!

Pick one day each week to be your "whatever you want" day. People are more successful when they feel like they are rewarding themselves. And you are no exception! If Sunday seems like the logical day for your free day because of family dinners, football games, movie night, then that will be your designated "off day." If Saturday is better because of date night, go for it.

Try to be consistent with your day off so that the other days in between can make up for the "free day." Occasionally you can switch them around, cause that's part of the fun of life, right?

You will also be surprised how much weight you will lose with this eating philosophy. You will shed the unwanted fat that your body doesn't need and get down to the size your body naturally wants to be. Not skinny, but not *Reubenesque* either. With the increase in metabolism and the increase in exercise, your body will release that excess you've been acquiring over these trying years. It takes time, but it's worth it. Your heart and your waistline will thank you!

In the Appendix I have given you some recipes to show you how easy and tasty eating clean, lean, unprocessed foods can be. Try some of the recipes and see what you think. And remember, a recipe is just a suggestion. Adapt them to your taste and to ingredients you prefer.

Your FEEDING YOUR BODY Declarations:

"I will commit to a clean, lean, natural food philosophy."
"I will buy organic whenever possible."
"I will not buy or eat processed foods."
"This will be my new food mind-set!"

Your FEEDING YOUR BODY Action Steps:

1. Buy only the leanest proteins you can find.
2. Buy organic everything when possible.
3. Don't buy processed foods. Period.
4. Take time to prep veggies for snacking and store in the refrigerator for convenience.
5. Take time to precook protein for easy access during the week.
6. Get used to the clean, lean flavors of your food.
7. Use as many extra veggies as possible in your dishes.
8. Use as many herbs and spices as possible in your dishes.
9. Experiment with new foods and seasonings.
10. Eat as many different colors as possible at each meal.
11. Commit to this eating philosophy.
12. Thank God for your New Life!

Step Five

I Is for INTELLIGENCE

It is important to address the feeding of your mind and soul.

Traveling, exploring, learning, and loving are all powerful ways of understanding our place in the universe, and connecting us with that one basic essence of life that binds us all together.

Opening yourself up to new cultures is incredibly enlightening. Learning to appreciate other ways of life helps you find your true place in the universe. You deepen your sense of humanity and the connection we all have when you witness other people's ways of living. Some bad, some good, but they all enrich your awareness of the importance of your own decisions in life.

Once you realize that you are no better or much different than most anyone else in this world, you become more tolerant, understanding, and compassionate. You are no better; you just might make different choices or be exposed to more options. And remember, it is not our place to judge other people, but to be responsible for our own decisions. There will always be extremists out there and should be considered so. But don't let them ruin your appreciation of the other people in this world that are basically the same as we are.

Traveling

Traveling is a fabulous way to learn to appreciate all the differences and similarities in this world. It's amazing to see how other countries have developed. The architecture, the cuisine, the art, the fashion . . . it's literally a whole new world. Anything from the public transportation to the way people greet each other is fascinating in other countries.

You will have to get over the fact that things are going to be different than you are used to at home. You wouldn't want things to be like home anyway, right? Why would you travel if that were the case? It is great fun going to Paris, sit on a park bench, and soak up the scenery. The people-watching is so rich. The ambiance is enchanting. Even the sounds are entertaining.

Or lying on a beach, looking at a sunset, counting all the colors of blue in the calm Caribbean. Or floating on your stomach in the clear ocean, looking at the sea life below you. Or gazing up from the top of a hill or mountain, watching the eagles soar.

Side bar: I recommend SCUBA diving highly! It's the closest thing to space travel we will get to experience in our lifetimes. Think about it... you are in a completely different world, where you are the visitor, zero gravity, and you can't even breathe on your own. Amazing! Talk about an experience! A must!

Pick your favorite country. The place you have always dreamed of visiting. And do it. Go! It's your turn! It will be the perfect way to clear your head and pave the way for your new life. Purge the old, welcome in the new.

Walking down the streets, riding a bike, taking a bus gives you a whole different perspective of the environment. Try to blend in. It's great fun. Buy an outfit there, wear it, sans the tourist tennis shoes, and see what it feels like to be a local. You get a whole different perspective and a lot more insight of the country and its people. You will be amazed.

Also, learn some of the language of the country you have chosen to explore. It will make all the difference in the world. Most people in other countries don't mind visitors from America at all, if you have the right attitude and show a little common courtesy. People who live in beautiful places like to share it with other people. But if you bring a "holier than thou" attitude, no one will want to deal with you. News flash: People at home don't want to deal with you either! That's how Americans have gotten a bad name in the traveling circles of the world. They tend to go to another country and expect it to be like home. It's not and shouldn't be.

When you travel, you should be appreciative and respectful of how other cultures have survived for centuries. Remember, America is the new kid on the block. Those other countries got along just fine before we ever came on the scene. And we will never change them anyway. Period. But we can learn a great deal from observing how others exist. We learn a great deal about ourselves, too. Just be selective of the places you chose and be prepared for what you will see.

Exploring

It's time to stretch yourself beyond your known limits. Push yourself outside of your comfort zone. Give yourself the thrill of a lifetime.

You can't achieve personal growth if you don't reach *past* your familiar boundaries and try something new.

I'm talking about skydiving, if you have the desire. Buy your first thong, and I don't mean the one that fits on your foot! Get a new hairstyle or color. Fly through the air with the greatest of ease . . . on a flying trapeze. Bungee jump off a bridge. Drive a race car around a track. Learn to SCUBA dive. Swim with dolphins, or sharks for that matter. Train for and run in a marathon.

Take cooking classes at Le Cordon Bleu in Paris. Take a biking tour through Italy. Go whitewater rafting in Colorado. Book a cruise, a singles one, maybe. Join a wine-tasting club. Become a public speaker on your specialty. Become an expert in something you love so you *can* become a public speaker. Whatever it is, do it!

You know what I'm talking about . . . something you've always wanted to do . . . but for some reason didn't. Well now is the time. It's your turn! And if you are limited by money, be creative with what you have access to in your area. There are a lot of things that don't cost money that would be outside of your normal existence and offer an exploring element. Stretching your boundaries will build self confidence and help you see the world through new eyes. And the thrill factor will be well worth it. Like I said, you can't grow if you don't push yourself.

Learning

It is important to always be learning *something*. Never let a day go by without learning something new. Like my mom says, "I consider the day lost if I haven't learned something."

Now I don't mean useless knowledge like who left whom or negative sensational news stories. I mean working on a new language, life skills, something intellectually stimulating. Whether it's trading your IRA, learning about art, taking music lessons, it's important to stretch yourself.

Don't let yourself get bored or *boring,* heaven forbid. It happens too easily--the proverbial "rut," as it were.

With this new attitude on life, you are primed to broaden your horizons. Become the kind of interesting person *you* admire. Exercise those synapses. Let them pop-pop-pop away. You will be stimulating new ideas and creative thoughts that will contribute to your goal of achieving your ***Dream Life***.

The creative process is fueled by processing new information. And you need new creative ways of accomplishing your ***Dream Life***. This process feeds itself and can be used in all aspects of your life. Fresh blood, creative ideas, new energy--these will lead you to your goal.

I personally think everyone should learn a second language. It promotes what I call "worldliness"--being world-friendly. How can we promote world peace if we can't communicate with at least one other culture? I mean really, let's take off the blinders and become a united world family. And this, along with traveling, is a good start. Yes, I am a romantic who thinks people should live in peace. No, I don't think it will ever totally happen as long as people are ruled by egos. But I can dream . . . .

I also think everyone should have a charity they contribute to. Whatever your situation is, if you are reading this book, you can afford to give back to the community. If not monetarily, then through time and effort. We have to lead and teach by example. If we don't work toward the greater good of humanity, then we are not accomplishing one of the most important jobs each of us was put on this earth to do.

Whether it is through your church, your local children's hospital, your child's school, or the Race for the Cure, everyone needs to contribute to the greater good. It's one of our spiritual purposes in life.

As for reading, there are so many interesting things to learn about. Books are a window to the world, especially if you have a limited budget. From finances, to food and wine, to spiritual enlightenment, there are some very gifted writers out there who have done most of the research for you. Take advantage of the abundance of knowledge offered to you.

Recommended readings:

- *Secrets of the Millionaire Mind* by T. Harv Eker
- *The New Earth: Awakening to Your Life's Purpose* by Eckhart Tolle
- *The Power of Now* by Eckhart Tolle
- *The Science of Success* by Wallace D. Wattles

- *Money and The Law of Attraction* by Esther and Jerry Hicks
- Anything by Suze Orman
- Anything by Erma Bombeck
- Anything by Peter Mayle
- Anything by Dr. Nicolas Perricone
- Anything about Julia Child (Love her!)
- Any cookbook (Love Jacques Pepin too!)
- *World Atlas of Wine* by Hugh Johnson and Jancis Robinson

Now, you add your list here . . . .

My list offers a variety of books to get you started. And it would be unending, if continued.

I always have an educational book, a cookbook, and an entertaining book going at any given time. I'm sure that says something about me, but I like to read different things when I'm in different moods. And I always have a French phrase book in my purse for downtime. This way I'm always prepared. OK, no comments, please!

Reading is truly an inexpensive way to broaden your horizons and learn something new without too much effort. It fits into anyone's schedule. Lunchtime, before bed, in the bathroom, on a beach . . . wherever.

Do this for you. Give yourself the gift of knowledge.

Loving

You need to realize that you don't need a man to complete you. Being dependent on someone to take care of you and having a loving partner to enjoy life with are two very different things. The stronger and more independent you are, the more you have to offer a relationship. Now is the time to focus on yourself and developing into the best you can be. When it's time, the right person will come along. But you can't force it. Just let it happen.

If you need to be in love, fall in love with *living*! In fact, fall in love with *living* anyway! It will be one of the best things you can do for yourself!

Start making it a priority to enjoy every day of your life. Do the things that you love to do. And when you have to do those annoying little necessities of life, even though you don't enjoy them, do them with a positive attitude. Might as well make the best of the situation. Am I right?

Your ***Dream Life*** needs to have a purpose and to be something that you *love* to do. It needs to be fulfilling and to make you happy. Your interactions with people need to have the same effect. Being in love with life can be your reality. You just have to embrace it and live it!

An important component to being in love with life is tapping into your spirituality. We all know by now that to find our inner peace, we have to connect with that life force that binds us all together. And we need it now more than ever. Feed your soul through exploring your spirituality. Whether it's through reading or worshiping, that inner peace is where your real personal power comes from. Nurture it.

You still need to appreciate men. No matter how badly you were burned, men and women were made for a reason. All procreating aside, it's the ying and yang thing. It's the salt and pepper, peanut butter and jelly, sun and moon thing. And it works, with the right person.

I don't want you to harden your heart, afraid to try again. Life is too short, and love can be so good! It's one of God's gifts to us, and we should enjoy it!

I still believe in the sanctity of marriage. I love the whole romantic concept. I was just married to the wrong person. So were you.

Eventually you will be ready to share your life again. And things will fall into place. You will make better choices next time. Just don't rush it.

Until then, focus on your ***Dream Life*** and making it a reality. Becoming self-sufficient will enable you to base your decisions for a mate on personality, not necessity. From this point on, you want to know that you don't need a partner for financial reasons, just for love.

During this healing process, you will learn the type of romantic life that you want the next time and what you will *not* tolerate. You will choose differently, more wisely. If you learned the lessons you needed to learn the first time around about relationships, the second time will be much better. Trust me. It will be worth the wait.

Think about it this way: The probability of marriages ending in divorce is higher today than ever, not to mention the divorce rate of second marriages. We are part of a whole new playing field. Making good decisions will increase our odds. And if we make our decisions based on fulfilling emotional needs and not financial ones, we are already ahead of the curve.

There are more men out there in our age range that are smarter and wiser, just like we are. Some of them have actually learned their lessons, just like we have. I can only hope that they will be more appreciative the next time around, like I will.

To address the issue of men our age wanting younger women, let them have 'em. That's not the type of man you want anyway. If they need a younger woman to feel younger or better about themselves, you don't need them. They haven't learned their lessons yet. Enough said.

Yes, there are still jerks out there, and that will never change. But go with your gut feeling. Usually you will be right. You know what's important now. The attributes you require will be easier to see. The nonsense you will not tolerate will also be easier to see.

Looks are fleeting, loyalty is lasting. Money comes and goes, being honorable and trustworthy remains. Those are inborn attributes that are at the core of a person's very being. And let's don't forget the importance of a sense of humor. We definitely need more of that in this world!

Some people take everything too seriously. I mean really! Lighten up! Choose to see the positive, entertaining side of life. There is enough bad out there without our trying to find it. If we spend our energy focusing on the fun, happy parts of life, we can give hope to others, not to mention to ourselves. We can lead by example. If you focus on the positive, you attract the positive. If you focus on the negative, you attract the negative.
Again, the Law of Attraction is there, whether you choose to acknowledge it or not. And the fact that you can control the energy that comes your way is so powerful. So choose very carefully what you focus on. And be consistent!

Happiness is a *choice.* It's how you *choose* to respond to life. *It's all in your control.* And that's what I've been talking about!

It's time to fall in love with living!

Your INTELLIGENCE Declarations:

"I will feed my mind and soul through traveling, exploring, learning, and loving!"
"I will learn to appreciate the differences in this world!"
"I will stretch myself beyond my comfort zone!"
"I will be open to love when the right person comes along!"
"I will fall in love with living!"

"It's My Turn!"

Your INTELLIGENCE Action Steps:

1. Start planning a trip to your dream destination. **Make it happen!**
2. Challenge yourself to do something new and exciting. You need the thrill.
3. Pick a foreign language and learn it. It's great fun.
4. Start learning about things that have always fascinated you.
5. Commit to reading something that will contribute to achieving your ***Dream Life***, or inner peace, or both.
6. Read whatever you want, just read.
7. Don't let yourself be calloused by your past experience with love. When you are ready, it will come. Until then, focus on you and making your ***Dream Life*** a reality!
8. Thank God for your New Life!

Step Six

S Is for SUCCESS

We've covered your changing the way you look and think about yourself.

We've covered how to live an energetic lifestyle.

We've covered how to choose having a positive attitude and enjoying life to its fullest.

We've covered how to feed your body with clean, lean, natural foods and how to make them taste fabulous.

We've also covered the importance of feeding your mind and soul through traveling, exploring, learning, and loving.

Now it's time to address your becoming the **Successful Woman** you were meant to be.

The CPR Approach

I recently read some great advice for becoming successful and happy. It was written by Jeff Herring, who calls himself "a recovering marriage and family therapist."

He said that in order to be successful at anything in life, you need to take the **"CPR Approach."**

CPR stands for **consistent**, **persistent,** and **resistant.**

Consistent--in our actions

Persistent--in our drive, and

Resistant--to setbacks and to all those who may tell us we can't do it!

How true is *that!* It's so hard to keep that determination and drive we initially build in ourselves to make important changes in our lives. Because *life* still happens and chisels away at our commitment when we are at our weakest.

When embarking on major changes, being consistent in our actions provides direction to our energy, being persistent provides momentum to our efforts, and being resistant to setbacks provides a grounding that keeps us on track.

It takes constant belief and trust in ourselves to build the momentum needed for change. It also takes *total commitment.* But it's hard to be totally committed to a goal when it's not clear in your mind.

Back to *visualizing* your ***Dream Life*** and exactly what it *looks* like.

When you have a clear picture of the kind of lifestyle and career you want to achieve, it becomes tangible. Real. Yours.

- What would make you want to get up in the morning with a *big* smile on your face?
- What would make you passionate about each day?
- What would make life worth living?

Answer these questions, and you've got your goal!

We are looking for excitement, purpose, and passion in these answers. We are looking for the reason you were born. We are looking for your true life path. Do you get where I'm going with this?

Think Big!
Live Big!
Be Big!

Your imagination is your only limitation. As I said before, don't edit your dream. Let it be as big as you've always seen it. Because if you can see it, you can achieve it.

Chuck R. Swindoll, who runs the website *Insight for Living* said, "We are all faced with a series of great opportunities brilliantly disguised as impossible situations." That's how I want you to consider your divorce. It's a great opportunity for you to finally be who you were always meant to be.

You just have to:

- **See the Dream!**
- **Live the Dream!**
- **Be the Dream!**

Make a plan how to accomplish this life you were meant to live, *work* the plan, and *live* the plan. You have to *totally embrace* the idea. *Totally* become that person. Cut off the *old* and live the *new*!

The clearer the image is in your mind, the closer you will be to designing a life well lived. Each day you need to be working toward your goal of success. Everything you do needs to direct you toward accomplishing that goal.

Ask the question, "Does this get me closer to accomplishing my goal?" If it does, do it and do it well. If it doesn't, don't do it! Period. Yes, I've said it before, but you need to be saying it *every day*!

You need to remember that what you focus on expands. Whether it is your *Dream Job* or your ***Dream Life***. The more energy you direct toward your goal, the sooner it will come into your existence.

Break down the requirements for your Dream Job. Research everything that needs to be acquired and in place for you to proceed. Learn everything you will need to know so that you start off as knowledgeable as possible. You don't have to know everything before you begin. You will *never* know everything. And a lot of it you can learn along the way.

If you wait until you think you know all there is to know about starting your new life, you will lose the momentum you've built from reading this book. And we don't want that!

If you are a planner, plan your finances accordingly. If you need a few months to save up for a rainy day, do so. You will feel more secure if things get lean during the start-up months. If you must, sell the old stuff you don't need from your *old* life, and use the money toward your *new* life. Ha! Take that!

What's important here is that you are being true to your self and your soul by tapping into your true life's purpose. Your ***Dream Life*** should fit that description. If it does, things will fall into place. The universe will start contributing to your success. People and relationships will come into your life that will contribute to your success.

And even though you are working toward a future goal, it is important to enjoy the everyday process of getting to that goal. Today is all we really have. We are no longer getting our identity from what has happened in the past. Today is when we choose to be positive, happy, and successful. If tomorrow never comes, we want to be sure that we made the most of today!

Learn what is needed to make a clear plan on how you will begin your new career and then jump in! Now is the best time to make this kind of change. You are already starting a new life socially, spiritually, and physically. What better time to start a new life career-wise? Just rip off the Band-Aid and go for it!

Think about how fabulous it will be when you are successful in your emotional life, your physical life, *and* your professional life. When you feel like you have established yourself as a confident, wise, and powerful force in this world.

You can do anything!

- You can contribute to the rest of the world in ways that feeds your soul.
- You can afford to do whatever you want, whenever you want.
- You can accomplish whatever goals you set for yourself.
- Because You are a **Successful Woman!**

Promise yourself that you will be *Consistent* in your actions, *Persistent* in your drive, and *Resistant* to setbacks.

And to hell with those who tell you you can't achieve your ***Dream Life!*** They don't know the **New You!**

Affirmations

Affirmations are statements of gratitude. You can't achieve your new goals if you don't appreciate the gifts you have right now. The idea behind affirmations is to reinforce the positive qualities you already have and encourage development of new qualities you want to possess.

Affirmations are three-part statements. The first part of your statement is being thankful for a quality you already possess. The second part is being thankful for a quality you are currently working on. The third part of the statement is being thankful for three qualities that you *want* to possess.

Example: "Thank you God for my health, thank you for my discipline, and thank you God for my courage, happiness, and success." or

"Thank you God for my intelligence, thank you for my wisdom, and thank you God for my determination, consistency, and courage."

Whatever traits you insert into the statement, they should be unique to *you*. Again, soul searching is in order. You are planting the seeds of success into your subconscious that will take you straight to your ***Dream Life.***

Recite this statement three times a day--every morning before your feet hit the floor, sometime midday when you can spend a couple of minutes to relax and concentrate on it, and the last thing you do in bed before you zone out. The goal is saying your affirmations often enough that it becomes your mantra. Then, when you wake up one day and feel you have accomplished those qualities, change your statement to fit the new goals you desire.

Like I've said earlier in the exercise section, when you are doing your cardio exercise is a great time to reinforce your affirmations. That repetition is exactly what you need to totally embed those goals into your whole being. You can never say them too often. What you focus on expands!

Affirmations are a constant reinforcement for positive personal growth. Again, our goal!

Being a Gracious Receiver

Another important aspect of being successful is being a good and gracious "receiver." Few things are as classy as a person who is a gracious receiver, someone who gracefully accepts gifts or compliments with style and true appreciation. Not arrogance, but genuine thankfulness.

You have been very blessed. You have gotten a new chance to live the life you've always wanted. You are luckier than most.

It is important that you appreciate the second chance you've been given and be grateful. There may have been times in your marriage, or life for that matter, that you were led to believe that you weren't worthy of gifts or compliments, that you were being selfish for wanting or getting things for yourself. Well, my friend, **THOSE DAYS ARE OVER!** I repeat: **THOSE DAYS ARE OVER! HALLELUJAH!**

There are many ways to become a good receiver. And a good way to start is by cleaning out the "old life" from your house and making room for your "new life." You don't have room for receiving new things if all of your old things are still in the way.

This is where the symbolic word "baggage" comes to mind.

That means all those closets that have years worth of stuff that you haven't wanted to deal with. The garage, under the deck, in the attic . . . need I go on?

Purging is part of the healing process. Out with the old, in with the new! You will even *breathe* better when the old stuff is gone.

This also applies to the men who have been in your life. You have to release the images of the old relationships so that you are open and receptive to new relationships. Sometimes this is the hardest thing to accomplish.

But you can do it. Anyone strong enough to create their successful new life can let go of the past. However, you have to deal with your old demons, it is mandatory for your growth that you do so. And remember, the longer you hold on to the past, the longer it will have power over you.

I recommend reading Eckhart Tolle's book *A New Earth: Awakening to Your Life's Purpose*. The power that comes from releasing the past and embracing the *now* will change your life. I wish this for you.

When you have cleaned out the cobwebs in your heart, like the closets in your house, you will be open and ready to receive. And when it comes your way, be gracious and appreciative.

Your SUCCESSFUL Declarations:

"I will be the **Successful Woman** I was meant to be!"
"I will accomplish my ***Dream Life***!"
"I will affirm my gifts and encourage my goals on a daily basis!"
"I will be a gracious receiver!"

Your SUCCESSFUL Action Steps:

1. Be *consistent* in your actions toward accomplishing your ***Dream Life***.
2. Be *persistent* in your drive to achieving your goals.
3. Be *resistant* to setbacks and to all those who tell you that you can't do it.
4. Research all the requirements for creating your Dream Job.
5. Be as knowledgeable as reasonably possible before you start.
6. Make a plan of action.
7. Work the plan with total commitment.
8. Embrace the new life you are working toward.
9. See it, live it, be it!
10. Get rid of the *old* so you have room for the *new*.
11. Thank God for your New Life!

Step Seven

H Is for HAPPY

You've made it! You've changed your life and your future! You are a **SELFISH WOMAN** who is powerful, successful, and most of all happy!

It's about time. You deserve it! You took control, and you made it happen. You are a phoenix that has risen out of the ashes of your old married life. You will forever be stronger, wiser, and more resilient.

You will never look at yourself the same way again. That was the *old* you. This is the ***New You!*** Be Happy with the New You! Be proud of what you've accomplished!

The *You* that is confident, radiant, and vivacious. The *You* that chooses to take control of her life. The *You* that can face *anything* now. The *You* that enjoys life to the fullest!

By now you realize that you don't have to be sad anymore. You can choose to be happy. It's all in your control. You can release the hold that your past has on you by forgiving yourself and those involved. Just let it go! Becoming a **SELFISH WOMAN** will bring you inner peace.

You can choose to set your default mode to ***Happy.*** You don't have to participate in other people's misery or chaos. Really, you don't! You don't have to live in that world anymore. I hope you have embraced that now.

How you choose to respond to what life dishes out shows your true character. Don't forget that. You know now that you can dictate whether you will come out on top or land in the bowels of hell. Busy--thanks though! Never again!

You have proven that you have the ability to create your ***Dream Life*** out of a miserable life. Now you have a proven tract record of success. You can accomplish anything you want badly enough! That, my friend, is true freedom!

I can not overly express the importance of being *"bien dans sa peau", or* comfortable in one's skin. Confidence is one of the most attractive things that a woman can possess. And with all the work you have done to become the woman you've always dreamed of being, this should be easy for you now. Totally comfortable with your self-image, your confidence in your ability to accomplish anything you want badly enough, and your command of your future. You've come a long way, Baby! (I couldn't help myself!)

Don't forget to surround yourself with beauty on a daily basis. Fresh cut flowers, scented candles, great music, flowering plants outside your windows, a fountain with running water on the porch. Puppies, cats, friends, family, whatever makes you happy. Constant positive reinforcement is important to maintaining a positive outlook, especially if it is not your normal mind-set. And it is beneficial even if it is your norm.

Side note: Try cloves and cinnamon sticks simmering in a pot of water on the stove. You will be amazed how great that is, especially in the fall and winter. The aroma is like a big hug.

The more we tap into our inner peace, the happier we are. That calm, warm, loved feeling that comes from our quiet, peaceful inner space keeps us in balance. And it is always there for you when you need it. You just have to remember to nurture it. And the more often you tap into that place, the easier it is to call it up in times of stress. Even if you just take ten minutes a day to sit quietly and listen to your soul, you will grow deeper in your connection with the larger power of the universe. We all have that place within ourselves, but not all of us remember it's there. It has always been there, quietly in the background of everything else that has been going on in your life. And the more often you go to that place, the stronger it becomes. And in turn, the stronger you become.

Stop reading the newspaper or watching the news on TV if it upsets you. Your reading or watching it doesn't change the events that have already happened. Our contributing to the forms of media that thrive on sensationalism condones their behavior, and in turn, perpetuates the madness. Stop watching negative shows on the TV or going to violent movies. If it gets our ratings, they will continue to make that trash. Again, we need to live and teach by example.

If you are in need of a little light humor, watch old *I Love Lucy* episodes or *Bewitched.* How great were those? Or be around funny friends. It will be good for your soul. Read some Dave Barry or Erma Bombeck. Nothing beats a hearty laugh.

And if you are in need of warming your soul, get out into nature. The breeze, the sound of birds, the flowing water, and the sun on your skin will do wonders for your attitude. If truly appreciated, it can help bring you back into balance. Staying in touch with nature is a way of staying connected to the spiritual world, which we all share. It's our daily reminder of the force that connects all living things. And we have easy access to it! Just walk outside. That connection with nature is one of the truest ways of feeling your inner peace.

Start taking pride in your accomplishments. You did it! You made your dream come true! You are better than you were before the divorce! This should definitely put a smile on your face!

Like I said, ***your divorce may be the best thing that ever happened to you!***

Make sure you continue your affirmations three times a day. It is important to keep reinforcing the ***New You***. Because *life* will continue to rear its little monstrous head and test your resolve. You need to stay committed to your *new life* and do what it takes to maintain control.

Don't forget Jeff Herring's CPR approach--be consistent in your actions, persistent in your drive, and resistant to setbacks and to all those who say it can't be done! Because *you* can do anything!

Now let's go over those affirmations again:

Thank you God for my (insert one of your current strengths), Thank you God for my (insert a trait you are not as strong at, but working on), And Thank you God for my (insert three strengths that you desire).

For example: "Thank you God for my health, thank you God for my discipline, and thank you God for my courage, determination, and success."

As your life changes, so do your affirmations. Adapt them to your current situation, and *chant, baby, chant!*

You just have to make affirmations a part of your daily routine. It will become second nature for you to chant them when you don't even realize it. At a stop light, in the checkout line, you will notice yourself quietly repeating your affirmations. How positive is that?

Happiness is contagious. A smile, a giggle, a kind word to the bag boy at the grocery store all contribute to a positive outlook on your life and those around you. The old saying is true, "What goes around, comes around." Kindness will come back to you tenfold. And even if it doesn't, it makes you feel better about the world.

A sure sign of a confident person is their ability to genuinely compliment others. In giving compliments to others, you are affecting their current state of being in a positive way. You are making someone feel good about themselves, even if only for a moment. And you will never know how that may affect the rest of their life. These seemingly small contributions to the betterment of this world do have a collective effect that you may never see. But if we all start spreading happiness, the exponential effect will be greater than we can imagine. If we want to change this world, we have to start one person at a time.

Happy people attract happy people. It's that simple. If you exude a bright, vivacious energy, it attracts other people who either have it or who want it in their lives. Your happiness can encourage others to choose to be happy also. It beats the hell out of the alternative, right!

And isn't that one of our goals--to surround ourselves with happy, positive, successful people who will contribute to our new life, not detract from it? It is hard to stay on tract if you are being derailed by the negative people around you. Don't let that happen. You've worked too hard to make your ***Dream Life*** your reality. Don't ever let anyone dictate your outcome again!

When you accept the role of leading by example, you really do have an effect on the people around you. If you can add even a little brightness into someone's life, you will also be feeding your own soul. You will be reinforcing all the positive things you've done to make yourself the ***Leading Lady in your own life!***

Your HAPPY Declarations:

"I am the confident, vivacious, and radiant woman I was always meant to be!"

"I am proud of the new me and the new life I have created for myself!"

"I am a powerful, successful, and wise woman who can handle anything!"

"I have made peace with my past and will never let it hold me back again!"

"I am *Happy* with the New Me!"

Your HAPPY Action Steps:

1. Reconnect with the spiritual force that binds all living things together!
2. Recite your affirmations three times a day, faithfully!
3. Surround yourself with happy, positive, successful people who will contribute to your new life and help you stay on tract.
4. Stop exposing yourself to negative influences, whether they be newspapers, TV, or people. Especially people!
5. Share your happiness and new outlook with others--you never know whose life you will influence for the better.
6. Apply CPR to your daily life--it works for everything!
7. Thank God for your New Life!

Lets Recap

At the beginning of this book, I told you I would teach you:

- how to release the old life and create a new, happier one
- how not to get paralyzed by the chaos of change
- how to give yourself permission to put *Yourself* first
- how not to listen to those old tapes, but make new, positive ones
- how to refuse to participate in the ugliness and negativity
- how to stay focused on the *New You*

I have given you permission to *forgive yourself* and to become the **Leading Lady in Your Own Life!**

Things I have helped you accomplished:

- You have forgiven yourself for what got you here in the first place--no judgment here, just help and hope.
- You have snapped yourself out of that *old* mind-set and have create a *new* outlook for your life.
- You have gotten rid of those *old* tapes in your head and made *new*, positive ones.
- You have released the power that the *old life* had on you and opened yourself up to being a gracious receiver of your *New Life*.
- You have realized that choosing a positive response to life is *all in your control!*
- You have learned how to visualize your ***Dream Life***, put details to that vision, and made that vision *your reality*.

- You have tapped into your vibrance through the feeding of your body, your mind, and your soul.
- You have embraced the importance of living an energetic lifestyle that brings out your true zest for life!

And don't forget how important it is to pamper yourself on a daily basis. Again, **You deserve it!**

Those days of feeling guilty and questioning your self-worth are **OVER!**
Those days of sadness and despair are **OVER!**
Those days of wondering if you will ever be happy again are **OVER!**

Now is the time to **Celebrate** your **New Zest for Life!**
Now is the time to **Revel** in your **New Power, Success,** and **Wisdom!**
Now is the time to **Share** the **New, Vibrant You with the World!**

You will never look at life the same way again. You will see the true beauty that life has to offer. You will embrace it and appreciate it. You will look forward to the new challenges that come your way.

You will realize that ***Your divorce was the best thing that ever happened to you!***

You are a **SELFISH WOMAN** who:
S--puts her needs and desires first because **IT'S YOUR TURN!**
E--lives an energetic lifestyle that makes her vibrant, vivacious, and dynamic!
L--chooses a positive attitude and enjoys life to the fullest!
F--feeds her body with clean, lean, unprocessed foods that energize her new life!
I--feeds her mind and soul through traveling, exploring, learning, and loving!
S--is now the successful, powerful force she was always meant to be!
H--is now happy with herself and the new life she has created!

CONGRATULATIONS!

I officially release you from your Old Life and welcome you to your NEW LIFE!

Go out into the world and be FABULOUS!

Be a Powerful, Successful Woman!

Be the Leading Lady in Your Life!

And most of all . . . Happy Living!

Appendix

Recipes--Here's What I'm Talking About

A few things to remember:

- a recipe is like a yellow street light . . . it's just a suggestion--if you like more of one thing and less of another, make the dish to your taste
- don't skip a recipe because you don't have every ingredient on the list; alter as needed
- also, I like my food well seasoned, so be forewarned and alter accordingly
- even if the recipe doesn't specifically call for it, assume every ingredient is organic whenever possible--just do it!
- if you cook onions and veggies long enough to get a little color on them (caramelizing), it will add more depth of flavor to your dish
- if you are using nonstick pots and pans, always preheat the pan over medium heat, never over high, and add the oil pretty quickly
- when using raw nuts, toast the nuts with dry heat as in a dry sauté pan or in a toaster oven to give the dish a deeper, more interesting flavor
- when a recipe calls for fresh herbs, the measurement is for after the herb is chopped, for example, 2 tablespoons fresh basil, chopped--means 2 tablespoons of basil after it is chopped.

Also, the first few recipes will have a list of the physical benefits that each ingredient offers. This is to drive home the importance of the effect food has on your body on a daily basis. After that, refer to the nutritional benefits in *Step Four - F is for Feeding you Body.*

TURKEY LETTUCE WRAPS

Serves 4 to 6

1 head romaine lettuce, cleaned and dried
2 tablespoons extra-virgin olive oil
1 pound ground turkey breast
1 can sliced water chestnuts, finely chopped
1 bunch scallions, finely chopped, about 6-8
1/2 red bell pepper, finely chopped
1 stalk celery, finely chopped
1 tablespoon chili flakes
3 tablespoons dry sherry
2 tablespoons light soy sauce
1 tablespoon toasted sesame oil
1 tablespoon oyster sauce

Sauce:
2 tablespoon plum sauce
1 tablespoon hoisin sauce
1 teaspoon soy sauce

In a wok, heat oil over medium heat, then add the ground turkey. Break up the meat while browning. After the meat is browned, add the chili flakes, water chestnuts, celery, red pepper, and onion and stir for about 2 minutes. In a small bowl, whisk the sherry, soy sauce, sesame oil, and oyster sauce together. Pour over the turkey mixture. Stir together for about 2 minutes; then remove from the heat.

The lettuce needs to be in pieces that are easy to either roll or be used as a "boat." You can either prefill the leaves and serve on a tray, or have a plate of lettuce leaves and a bowl of the turkey mixture on the table, and let them go at it. Have the sauce and chili oil at the ready for serving. They are both yummy additions.

For the sauce, mix the ingredients with 2 tablespoons of water and pour in a bowl.

An alternative for the romaine lettuce is iceberg. Clean the leaves and serve piled on a plate. Grass-fed ground beef or lean ground pork are good substitutes for turkey.

Add a bowl of brown rice to the table for the perfect healthy, interactive meal.

Benefits:

- leafy greens, like romaine lettuce--protect against macular degeneration; heart healthy; lowers cholesterol and blood pressure; provides moisture to skin
- extra-virgin olive oil--antioxidant; heart healthy; lowers bad cholesterol; raises good cholesterol; decreases blood pressure; protects against colon cancer; helps keep arteries dilated
- turkey breast--promotes healthy skin; aids in metabolizing energy and fats; promotes healthy gastrointestinal tract and nervous system; helps protect against certain cancers; helps promote bone density; has cancer-fighting antioxidants
- scallions/onions--cancer fighting, protect against prostate and esophageal cancer; builds strong bones; antioxidants; anti-inflammatory, antibiotic, and antiviral properties; protects against cancer and heart disease; relieves asthma and hay fever symptoms; lowers blood pressure
- bell peppers--all colors--low in calories and high in vitamins and minerals; protects against lung cancer and promotes bone health
- celery--appetite control, stems carb cravings; aids in digestion; lowers blood pressure; increases blood flow; lowers stress levels; helps renew joints, bones, arteries, and all connective tissue; inhibits tumor growth
- chili pepper flakes--same benefits as hot peppers--promotes eye health; remedy for cough and colds; lowers bad cholesterol; pain reliever; enhances circulation, boosts metabolism and increases body temperature; aids in digestion and kills bad bacteria in stomach; used for healing in Ayurvedic (traditional India) medicine.

TURKEY TOMATO PASTA

Serves 4 to 6

1 1/4 pounds ground turkey breast
3 garlic cloves, minced
1/2 onion, chopped
2 tablespoons extra-virgin olive oil
1 red bell pepper, finely chopped
1 stalk celery, finely chopped
1 carrot, finely chopped
6- to 8-ounce can organic tomato paste
28-ounce can fire-roasted diced tomatoes
2 teaspoons dried oregano
2 teaspoons freshly ground pepper
2 teaspoons sea salt + 2 tablespoons for pasta water
1 cup red wine--merlot or cabernet
1/2 cup grated Parmesan
1 pound whole wheat pasta--spaghetti or fettucini
2 tablespoons flat leaf parsley, chopped

Brown the turkey and onions in olive oil over medium heat, adding 1 teaspoon salt, the oregano, and 1 teaspoon black pepper. After the browning is halfway done, add the celery and carrots; then after the turkey is completely browned, add the garlic. Let it cook for about a minute; then stir in the tomato paste and let cook for 2 more minutes. Now stir in the canned tomatoes and wine to simmer for at least 30 minutes.

While the sauce is simmering, bring a pot of salted water to a boil. Add the pasta when the water is at a rapid boil and cook per instructions on box. When the pasta is al dente (slightly firm to the tooth), drain, pour into a serving bowl and toss with sauce. Sprinkle top with 1/2 cup grated Parmesan. It's also good sprinkled with flat leaf parsley and crushed red pepper (remember your metabolism!).

Benefits:

- turkey breast--promotes healthy skin; aids in metabolizing energy and fats; promotes healthy gastrointestinal tract and nervous system; protects against certain cancers; promotes bone density; antioxidant

- extra-virgin olive oil--antioxidant; heart healthy, lowers bad cholesterol; raises good cholesterol; decreases blood pressure; protects against colon cancer; helps keep arteries dilated
- garlic--antioxidant; antiviral, antibacterial, antimicrobial, and antiparasitic properties; lowers bad cholesterol without lowering the good; reduces plaque in arteries; prevents platelets in blood from sticking together; cancer fighting; helps prevent common cold
- onions--cancer fighting; protects against prostate and esophageal cancer; builds strong bones; antioxidant; anti-inflammatory, antibiotic, and antiviral properties; protects against heart disease; relieves asthma and hay fever symptoms; lowers blood pressure
- bell peppers--all colors--low in calories and high in vitamins and minerals; protects against lung cancer and promotes bone health
- celery--appetite control; stems carb cravings; aids in digestion; lowers blood pressure; increases blood flow; lowers stress levels; helps renew joints, bones, arteries, and all connective tissue; inhibits tumor growth
- carrots--antioxidants; protects against bladder, cervical, prostate, colon, larynx, esophageal, and postmenopausal breast cancer; inhibits tumor growth; protects eyes; helps prevent macular degeneration and cataracts; immune system stimulator
- tomatoes--cancer fighting; helps reduce blood pressure; helps reduce risk of heart attacks; helps prevent atherosclerosis; disease fighting; helps prevent macular degeneration
- oregano--the herb with the highest antioxidant activity; antifungal, antibacterial, anti-parasitic, anti-inflammatory, antimutagenic, anticarcinogenic properties; digestive aid; supports joint function
- black pepper--increases circulation
- red wine--rich in antioxidants; helps protect against cancers; improves blood flow to the brain and helps prevent blood clots; protects the heart; supports health; has anti-aging properties
- parsley--aids detoxification; inhibits tumors; cancer fighting; protects eyes; builds strong bones; anti-inflammatory and antibacterial properties; benefits kidneys and tissue renewal.

TURKEY CHILI

Serves 4 to 6

2 tablespoons extra-virgin olive oil
1/2 white onion, chopped
1 leek, chopped, white and light green part only
1 1/4 pound ground turkey breast
15-ounce can fire roasted diced tomatoes
15-ounce can Rotel tomatoes
15-ounce can kidney beans, drained
6-ounce organic tomato sauce
15-ounce can hominy, drained
1/2 cup strong brewed coffee or 1 tablespoon dried coffee granules
1 tablespoon Worcestershire sauce
sea salt
freshly ground pepper
2 tablespoons cumin
2 tablespoons chili powder
1 tablespoon dried thyme

Sauté the onions and leeks in the olive oil over medium heat. After about 5 minutes, add the ground turkey and cook thoroughly, breaking into small pieces as it browns. Add 1 teaspoon of both salt and pepper, 1 tablespoon each of the cumin, thyme, and chili powder as the turkey cooks. This toasts the spices and infuses the taste into the turkey, which is the key to cooking with ground turkey.

After the turkey is completely cooked, add the rest of the ingredients, including the rest of the seasonings; stir and simmer for 20 minutes.

Taste for seasoning and serve. Dill pickles, chili flakes, pickled jalapeños, and grated cheddar cheese are all good accompaniments with this chili. It also looks cool to serve the chili in iceberg lettuce leaves as your bowl with slices of avocado on the top.

Benefits:

- extra-virgin olive oil--antioxidant; heart healthy; lowers bad cholesterol and raises good cholesterol; decreases blood pressure; protects against colon cancer; helps keep arteries dilated

- onions and leeks--cancer fighting; protects against prostate and esophageal cancer; builds strong bones; antioxidant; anti-inflammatory, antibiotic, and antiviral properties; protects against heart disease; relieves asthma and hay fever symptoms; lowers blood pressure
- turkey breast--promotes healthy skin; aids in metabolizing energy and fats; promotes healthy gastrointestinal tract and nervous system; protects against certain cancers; promotes bone density; antioxidant
- tomatoes--cancer fighting; reduces blood pressure; reduces risk of heart attacks; helps prevent atherosclerosis; fights disease; helps prevent macular degeneration
- beans--lowers risk of cancer, heart disease, diabetes, and obesity; lowers cholesterol; regulates blood sugar and insulin; inhibits cancer cell reproduction and growth of tumors
- coffee--increases antioxidants in the blood; increases mental alertness and physical stamina
- black pepper--increases circulation
- cumin--improves digestion and relieves heartburn; relieves allergies; protects against breast, stomach, and liver cancers; helps detox the liver; promotes energy production and metabolism; supports immune system
- chili powder--same benefits as hot peppers; promotes eye health; remedy for cough and colds; lowers bad cholesterol; pain reliever; enhances circulation; boosts metabolism and increases body temperature; aids in digestion and kills bad bacteria in stomach; used for healing in Ayurvedic medicine
- thyme--powerful antiseptic, antioxidant, anti-inflammatory; aids in digestion; relieves chest and respiratory problems
- avocados--antioxidant; lowers cholesterol; protects the prostate; reduces risk of cancer and diabetes; protects against heart disease; helps eyes and skin stay healthy.

WILD COD FILLET with COCONUT VEGGIES

Serves 2

2 6-ounce fresh wild cod fillets
2 tablespoons coconut oil
1/2 red bell pepper, julienned (cut into thin, long slices)
1/2 green bell pepper, julienned
1/2 onion, julienned
1 cup cherry tomatoes, halved
sea salt and freshly ground pepper to taste
sprinkling of green chili habanero seasoning

Melt the coconut oil in a skillet over medium heat. Add the onions and sauté for 2 minutes. Sprinkle the cod fillets with sea salt, pepper, and the seasoning. Add the fillets to the middle of the skillet, with the onions pushed to the sides. Now add the rest of the red and green bell peppers to the onions and simmer for 5 minutes.

Turn the fillets and add the tomatoes. Simmer for another 5 minutes. Remove from the skillet.

Serve the veggies over the fish; then sprinkle with fresh lemon juice.

Divine! Yummy buttery flavor, and no butter added!

GOLD MINE GAZPACHO

Serves 10 to 12

Truly the best Gazpacho ever and so full of antioxidants, it's a gold mine! The olives and feta option are inspired by Ina Garten, the Barefoot Contessa. Ingenious touch. Makes approx. 12 cups or servings.

2 cups leftover ciabatta or country bread, crust removed and cubed
3 large garlic cloves, chopped
3 tablespoons fresh oregano, chopped or 1 tablespoon dried
3 tablespoons Italian parsley, chopped
3 tablespoons extra-virgin olive oil
3 tablespoons red wine vinegar

1 yellow or orange bell pepper, chopped
1 red bell pepper, chopped
1 small red onion, chopped
1 seedless cucumber, seeded (there will still be seeds) and chopped
4 large or 6 smaller tomatoes, chopped
1/2 cup kalamata olives, pitted
46-ounce organic tomato juice
2 teaspoons sea salt
1 teaspoon freshly ground black pepper
1 firm avocado, cubed

In the bowl of a food processor, mix the bread, garlic, oregano, and parsley until the texture is a fine consistency. Then add the oil and vinegar and process until smooth. Pour into a large mixing bowl.

In separate batches, chop each of the peppers, onion, cucumber, tomatoes, and olives in the processor and pour into the large mixing bowl. Stir in the bread mixture. Then add the tomato juice, salt, and pepper and stir completely. Refrigerate for a few hours so the flavors can merge.

Just before serving, top each bowl with avocado cubes. Another serving option is crumbled feta cheese on top of each bowl. It gives the soup additional color, as well as a heartiness. But the soup is fabulous with or without the cheese.

LENTIL and SPINACH SOUP

Serves 8 to 10

1 white onion, chopped
1 leek, white and light green parts, chopped
1 large garlic clove, chopped
2 tablespoons extra-virgin olive oil
1 pound dried lentils, washed (check for stones)
2 carrots, diced
2 celery stalks, diced
28-ounce can organic tomatoes, chopped
16 ounces fresh or frozen chopped organic spinach, chopped
8 cups organic chicken stock

2 large bay leaves or 3 medium size
1 teaspoons freshly ground black pepper
2 teaspoons ground sage
1 tablespoon sea salt

In a large pot, warm oil over medium heat. Add the onions and leeks, and sauté for 5 minutes. Then add the garlic, letting it heat up for about a minute. Add lentils, carrots, celery, and stock, giving it a good stir. Add your bay leaf, black pepper, and sage and let cook for 1 1/2 hours. Now add your tomatoes, spinach, and salt. Simmer 10 more minutes. Adjust the seasoning as needed.

Variations: Use Rotel tomatoes instead of plain, or use fire-roasted tomatoes and dried thyme instead of sage--great!

This dish can also be made as a side dish by adding approximately 2 cups less of the stock. Make sure it doesn't get dry.

This soup can be served as is or can be thickened by using an immersion blender, removing the bay leaf first.

This soup is very low in fat and high in nutrients.

You can keep half for serving and put half in your freezer for a busy night, or just make half the recipe for a one-time serving. For a real treat, stir in thinly sliced aged provolone or grated Parmesan cheese. Fantastic!

PEA and MINT SOUP

Serves 4 to 6

2 tablespoons extra-virgin olive oil
1 medium onion, thinly sliced
4 cups chicken stock
1 teaspoons sea salt
16 ounces frozen petite green peas
1 cup fresh mint leaves, loose
7-ounce container 2% Greek yogurt
1 tablespoon unsalted butter
1 tablespoon Tabasco sauce, or to taste

1 teaspoon sugar, optional

In a large sauce pan, heat the oil over medium heat. Add the onions and sauté for about 5 minutes, stirring so they won't get brown. Then add the stock and salt and bring to a boil. Add the peas and all but a few leaves of the mint and bring back to a boil. Let that boil for about 3-5 minutes; then turn off the heat.

With an immersion blender, puree the mixture to desired smoothness. You can also puree this in batches in a blender for a smoother consistency. While pureeing, add the yogurt and butter. If the peas are not sweet, add the sugar, stir, taste for seasoning, and serve. Garnish with a dollop of yogurt and a mint leaf.

This makes a great first course, or serve as a lunch with a salad or a sandwich.

WHITE BEANS, SPINACH, and TOMATOES

Serves 4 to 6

2 tablespoons extra-virgin olive oil
1 onion, chopped
1 garlic clove, chopped
2 cans white beans
1 can Rotel tomatoes
15-ounce can fire-roasted organic diced tomatoes
10-ounce bag frozen organic spinach, or one bunch fresh, cleaned
1 teaspoon chili flakes
1 tablespoon dried oregano
sea salt and freshly ground black pepper

Sauté onions in the warmed olive oil over medium heat for about 5 minutes. Sprinkle with a pinch of sea salt and pepper. Then add the garlic and cook for another minute, stirring often so the garlic won't burn. If you add the chili flakes when cooking the onions, it will give the dish more spice. Otherwise, add the chili flakes, white beans, tomatoes, and oregano after the first 5 minutes. Add another pinch of salt and pepper and let it all simmer for at least 5 more minutes. Then add the spinach and continue to simmer for 10 more minutes.

Taste for seasoning and serve.

CREAM of MUSHROOM SOUP

Serves 4 to 6

1 tablespoon extra-virgin olive oil
2/3 stick of organic unsalted butter
2 leeks, finely chopped white and light green parts
1 white onion, chopped
1 stalk celery, finely chopped
1 large carrot, finely chopped
5 stems of fresh thyme
10 ounces fresh cremini mushrooms, chopped
4 ounces dried mixed wild mushrooms, rehydrated in 2 cups hot water for 20 minutes
1/2 teaspoon cayenne
1/4 cup whole wheat flour
1 cup dry white wine
4 cups filtered water
2/3 cup organic half and half
1 1/4 teaspoons sea salt
1/2 teaspoon freshly ground pepper

Melt the butter in the olive oil over medium heat. Add the leeks, onion, carrots, celery, thyme sprigs, and a pinch of salt and sauté for at least 10 minutes, letting the vegetables soften.

Remove the mushrooms from the rehydrating water and reserve the liquid. Chop the mushrooms and add to the pot. Also add the fresh mushrooms, which have been cleaned and sliced, along with another pinch of salt and fresh ground black pepper. Let the mixture simmer another 15 minutes. Now add the reserved liquid from the mushrooms (being careful not to include the grit at the bottom of cup) and the white wine to the pot, simmering for another 15 minutes.

It's time to add the flour, stirring it in and cooking for at least 3 more minutes. Now add 4 cups of filtered water, cayenne pepper, and simmer for 15 more minutes.

The soup should have an earthy, yummy aroma by now. Take out the thyme stems before stirring in the half and half. The soup is great just as it is, but it will be velvety if you puree it with an immersion blender or in small batches in a regular blender. Taste for seasoning, and enjoy!

HEAL THYSELF SOUP

Serves 8 to 10

3 tablespoons extra-virgin olive oil
3 tablespoons organic unsalted butter
1 large leek, chopped
1 onion, chopped
2 garlic cloves, chopped
3 carrots, chopped
3 celery stalks, chopped
15-ounce can organic white beans, drained
8 ounces frozen organic lima beans
15-ounce can Rotel tomatoes
28-ounce can organic fire-roasted tomatoes
6 cups filtered water
4 handfuls of organic fresh baby spinach leaves
1 tablespoon dried thyme
1 tablespoon dried oregano
1 teaspoon freshly ground pepper
2 teaspoons sea salt

Heat the oil and butter over medium flame. Add the leeks and onions and sauté until the onions start to brown. Then add the garlic and cook another minute. Now add the carrots, celery, beans, thyme, oregano, bay leaves, sea salt, and pepper. Stir together and cook for about 5 minutes or until the veggies get a little color on them. Then add the water, stir, and bring to a boil. Now lower the heat and simmer for about 45 minutes. Add the tomatoes and cook for 10 more minutes. Add the handfuls of fresh spinach, stir, simmer 5 more minutes.

Taste for seasoning and serve.

Notes:

- if you will caramelize (cook until brown) the onions and leeks first, you will add a depth of flavor to the soup
- organic white beans are fine from a can
- using beans in a can take less time to soften than frozen ones, so give the frozen beans time to soften before adding the salt
- I prefer fire-roasted tomatoes because they add a depth of flavor, and the whole tomatoes are of better quality than those diced, chopped, or pureed
- when using the dried herbs, either use a handheld spice grinder or rub the herbs in your hands first to release the oils and make them taste livelier
- add more water if the liquid level gets too low.

BEEF STEW

Serves 6 to 8

3 tablespoons extra-virgin olive oil
1 1/2 pounds grass-fed organic lean stew meat
1 white onion, chopped
2 garlic cloves, minced
1 sweet potato, chopped
3 carrots, chopped
3 celery stalks, chopped
2 cups baby lima beans
28-ounce can fire-roasted tomatoes
3 bay leaves
1 teaspoon dried thyme or 1 tbs. fresh thyme
1 teaspoon freshly ground black pepper
2 teaspoons sea salt, more if needed to taste, but not until cooking is done
5 cups water

Now is the time to experiment with whatever veggies are in the refrigerator. Even bagged lettuce goes good in this soup.

Heat the oil over medium heat, in a large soup pot. When the oil starts to shimmer, add the meat. Sprinkle with 1 tsp. salt while sautéing. Turn after 3 minutes or when the first side is brown; then let the meat brown on other side. Your goal is to seal the surface of each side of the meat to retain its juices. Add the onions, stir and sauté for 3 more minutes. Next add the garlic and cook for 3 minutes, stirring so the garlic won't burn. Now add the rest of the veggies, the water, the bay leaves, thyme, pepper, and the other teaspoon of salt and bring to a boil. Turn down the heat and simmer for about 30 minutes and voila! Health in a bowl!

BROCCOLI with TOASTED ALMONDS

Serves 4

1/4 cup toasted almonds, chopped
1 large head of broccoli florets, separated
2 tablespoons extra-virgin olive oil
1 large shallot, finely chopped
1/4 teaspoon red chili flakes
1/4 cup fresh red bell pepper, finely chopped
1 tablespoon fresh dill, chopped
1 lemon, juiced
sea salt and freshly ground black pepper to taste

Toast whole almonds with skins in a toaster oven at 350 degrees for about 15 minutes, depending on how toasted you like them. Set aside to cool.

Place the separated broccoli florets in a bamboo steamer over a sauté pan of boiling salted water. Steam the broccoli until tender; then set aside.

Heat a sauté pan on a medium setting. Add the oil and heat until it shimmers. Then add the shallots and chili flakes and cook for about a minute, letting the shallots soften but not burn. Add the florets and toss to coat each floret with oil and shallots.

Turn the heat off. Sprinkle the fresh dill and lemon juice, the chopped toasted almonds, and red bell pepper over the florets and toss again. Salt and pepper to taste.

Can be served warm, at room temperature, or cold.

TZATZIKI

Serves 10 to 12

16 ounces Greek yogurt, full fat
1 hothouse cucumber, skin on and grated
1 tablespoon plus 1/2 teaspoon sea salt
1/2 cup sour cream
1 tablespoon white wine vinegar
juice of 1 small lemon
1 tablespoon extra-virgin olive oil
2 garlic cloves, minced
2 tablespoons fresh dill, chopped
1/4 teaspoon freshly ground black pepper

Put the grated cucumber in a sieve and stir in 1 tablespoon salt, then place over a bowl. Let the water drain out of the cucumbers for at least 2-3 hours.

Place the yogurt and sour cream in a bowl. Mix in the drained cucumber, vinegar, lemon juice, oil, garlic, dill, and salt and pepper. Taste for seasoning, and it's ready to serve.

Tzatziki can be used in all kinds of creative ways. Dressing for salads, instead of mayo for sandwiches, dip for veggies and chips . . . insert ideas here.

BLACK BEAN SALSA

Serves 6 to 8

2 cans organic black beans, drained and rinsed
1/2 red bell pepper, small diced
1 large fresh jalapeño, seeded and minced
1/2 medium red onion, minced
40 cherry or grape tomatoes, quartered
1 avocado, diced
3 tablespoons fresh cilantro, chopped
1 1/2 teaspoons sea salt
1/2 teaspoon freshly ground black pepper

1/2 teaspoon dried ground cumin
1/4 + 1/8 cup fresh Meyer's lemon juice

Mix all the ingredients in a large bowl. Taste for seasoning. Don't stir too much or the avocado will disintegrate. Cover and refrigerate overnight. Flavors will mature and be fabulous the next day.

Serve with baked chips.

BLACK BEAN and AVOCADO SALAD

Serves 6 to 8

This is a variation of the above recipe.

1 can black beans, rinsed
2 jalapeño peppers, seeded, deveined, and minced
1 yellow or orange bell pepper, diced
1/2 cup red onion, minced
1 pint cherry tomatoes, halved
1 tablespoon fresh cilantro, chopped
zest of 2 limes
2 large avocados, diced
lime vinaigrette:
juice of 2 limes, more if needed
1/4 cup extra-virgin olive oil
1 teaspoon salt
1/2 teaspoon pepper
1/4 teaspoon cayenne
1 large garlic clove, minced

In a large bowl, mix the black beans, jalapeño, yellow pepper, onion, and tomatoes together. In a smaller bowl, whisk the vinaigrette together, and pour over the salad and toss. Add the avocados just before serving and toss again, so the avocados won't turn brown or disintegrate. Taste for seasoning. Chill until ready to serve.

HEIRLOOM TOMATO and AVOCADO SALAD

Serves 4 to 6

This recipe is to encourage you to think outside the box. Start putting foods together that you like, by layering them, mixing them together, or by putting one inside the other. You could chop up everything but the avocado, put it into the cavity of the avocado, then sprinkle with the lemon juice and lay on top of the heirloom tomato slice. Or you could lay the ingredients into a leaf of romaine lettuce and serve as an open-faced sandwich. Beautiful!

2 large heirloom tomatoes, reddish
1/2 avocado, or more depending on size of tomatoes, sliced
6 basil leaves, torn into small pieces
sea salt and freshly ground pepper
sprinkle of dried oregano, rubbed between your fingers
squeeze of fresh lemon juice
romaine lettuce leaves

Slice the heirloom tomatoes onto a serving plate. I like the big reddish ones with lots of creases, like it's gathered up at the end. Sprinkle a little salt and pepper over the top. Then sprinkle some of the basil pieces evenly onto the tomatoes. Now lay the avocado slices onto the tomatoes, sprinkle with a little salt, pepper, and a squeeze of lemon juice. Top with a little more basil pieces. Serve at room temperature or chilled. Make sure the avocado is covered with the lemon juice so that it won't turn brown.

To serve on individual plates, put a lettuce leaf under the tomato, so that you get the nutrients of the dark green leafy vegetable.

An alternative is to add slices of fresh mozzarella as a layer. Yummy!

STUFFED SWEET BABY PEPPERS

Serves 6 to 8

24 small sweet peppers, can be multicolors
1/2 medium white onion, finely chopped
bunch chives, chopped

2 tablespoons parsley, chopped
6 ounces neufchatel cream cheese
1/2 cup Parmesan cheese, grated
1/2 cup petite green peas, thawed
6 slices apple-smoked bacon, cooked crispy, chopped in small pieces
1/2 teaspoon sea salt
1/4 teaspoon freshly ground pepper
olive oil cooking spray

Cut the stem end of each pepper and clean out the inside with a paring knife. Be careful not to cut the walls of the pepper. Put them aside.

Chop the bacon in small pieces, and cook over medium heat until crispy. Remove from skillet with slotted spoon and drain on paper towels. Wipe out the pan, add 2 tablespoons extra-virgin olive oil, and cook the onions until caramelized (browned) about 5-7 minutes. Drain the onions on a paper towel to remove excess fat. Let the bacon and onions cool.

In a bowl, mix the onions, chives, cream cheese, Parmesan, peas, and bacon. Stir in salt and pepper. Mix thoroughly. Taste for seasoning and adjust.

With a small spoon, fill the cavity of each pepper with the cheese mixture, making sure it gets down into each one.

These peppers can be served raw at room temperature, or can be heated for about 10 minutes in a 350-degree oven on a cookie sheet that has been sprayed with the cooking spray. The cheese will get warm, and the peppers will still have a little crunch.

GREEK STUFFED BELL PEPPERS

Serves 6 to 8

2 tablespoon extra virgin olive oil
1 1/4 pound 96% lean grass-fed ground beef
1 white onion, finely chopped
2 garlic cloves, minced
4 ounces mushrooms, finely chopped
2 large handfuls of fresh arugula, chopped

3 ounces organic tomato paste
1 teaspoon chili flakes
1 tablespoon dried oregano
3 ounces Greek pickled peppers (6-7 peppers), chopped
1/3 cup kalamata olives, chopped
5 ounces crumbled feta cheese
6-8 multicolored bell peppers (depending on the size of peppers), de-stemmed, seeds and veins cored out without cutting through the body of the peppers
sea salt and freshly ground pepper to taste

Preheat the oven to 350 degrees.

Cut the top stem end out of the pepper, along with the seeds and veins. Wash inside and out and set aside.

Heat the olive oil over medium flame. Add the onions and sauté for at least 5 minutes. Then add the beef and start browning until halfway done. Add the garlic, mushrooms, oregano, salt and pepper, and chili flakes. Continue cooking until the meat is thoroughly cooked.

Turn off the heat and add the arugula, olives, Greek peppers, and feta cheese. Mix thoroughly. Taste for seasoning.

Stand up the pepper shells in a casserole dish so that they are tightly positioned and won't fall over. Fill each cavity with the meat mixture.

Bake in preheated oven for 15-18 minutes. Let stand for 10 minutes.

Options: Sun-dried tomatoes, toasted pine nuts

CARROTS with DILL

Serves 4 to 6

2 pounds organic carrots, sliced diagonally
1 large shallot, diced
2 tablespoons extra-virgin olive oil
1 tablespoon fresh dill, chopped
1/2 lemon, juiced
sea salt and freshly ground pepper to taste

Put the sliced carrot pieces in a tray of a bamboo steamer, cover with lid, and place over a skillet of boiling, salted water. Steam the carrots for about 10 minutes. You want the carrots to still have a slight firmness. Take the steamer off the skillet and set aside.

Rinse out the skillet and dry. Put the skillet over medium heat, then add the extra-virgin olive oil. When oil is shimmering, stir in the shallots. Continue to stir for about a minute as the shallots soften and release their aroma. Then add the steamed carrots and toss together, coating each piece of carrot with the oil and shallots. Remove from heat and sprinkle on the fresh dill, salt and pepper to taste, and combine. The final touch is squeezing the juice of half a lemon. Toss together and enjoy!

This dish is good warm, at room temperature, or cold.

CREOLE SEASONING

Makes about 2 cups

2 tablespoons dried oregano
1/3 cup + 1 tablespoon sea salt
1/4 cup granulated garlic
1/4 cup freshly ground black pepper
1/3 cup cayenne pepper
2 tablespoons dried thyme
1/3 cup + 1 tablespoon paprika
3 tablespoons granulated onion

Combine all ingredients and mix thoroughly. Pour into glass jar that has tight lid. Makes 2 cups. Will last in the pantry for at least 6 months.

Great as a gift; put in a flip-top decanter. Attach instructions, which are to sprinkle on fish fillets, shellfish, poultry, or pork. Drizzle with fresh lemon juice and olive oil and let marinate for 10-15 minutes; then cook as desired. No additional seasoning needed.

Can also be added sparingly to tzatziki, cheese sauce, and white sauces.

HERBES de PROVENCE

Makes about 2 cups

1/4 cup dried leaf thyme
1/4 cup dried leaf savory
1/4 cup dried leaf marjoram
1/4 cup dried leaf oregano
1/8 cup dried rosemary
1/8 cup dried sage
1/8 cup fennel seeds

Mix together and store in an airtight container for up to 6 months.

Fabulous on fish, pork, steak, and roasted or grilled veggies, you name it!

ITALIAN HERB MIX

Makes about 1 1/2 cups

2 tablespoons granulated garlic
2 tablespoons crushed red pepper flakes
2 tablespoons freshly ground black pepper
2 tablespoons kosher salt or course sea salt
1 tablespoon dried rosemary
3 tablespoons dried oregano
3 tablespoons dried basil
3 tablespoons dried parsley

Mix the herbs into an airtight jar for storage. Serve sprinkled in olive oil as a dipping oil for bread; roll goat cheese log in mixture and serve with baguette; season scrambled eggs, roasted vegetables, or any way you can think of.

BLUEBERRY and PEACH SORBET

Makes 3 quarts

2 cups frozen organic blueberries
1 cup frozen organic peaches
1 1/2 cups organic cranberry juice cocktail
3/4 cup organic raw agave nectar
1/4 teaspoon cinnamon
juice of 1/2 lemon

Puree ingredients in blender until smooth. Pour into frozen bowl of ice cream maker and churn for about 25 minutes, or until desired consistency.

Spoon into freezer proof container and keep in freezer until ready to serve.

PINEAPPLE in DARK RUM SAUCE

Serves 6 to 8

1 pineapple peeled, cored, and sliced in half moons
drizzle of organic honey
3-4 tablespoons dark rum
1 lime, zested, then juiced
sprinkle of cinnamon

Place the peeled pineapple in a casserole dish, drizzle with the honey, dark rum and lime juice, then sprinkle the lime zest over the top. Marinate for at least 30 minutes.

Place enough pineapple for an individual serving on a plate and spoon over some sauce. Put a dollop of marscapone cheese or creme fraiche in the middle, sprinkle with a little cinnamon, top with a piece of mint, and Voila!

Variation:

- dark maple syrup instead of the honey and dark rum
- don't add dairy if you are lactose intolerant
- don't forget the cinnamon!

Now, after seeing the physical benefits of food, you cannot deny the power of Mother Nature!

If you change your diet, you change your life!

Resources

Ahem, Leslie, and Paul Antokolsky. "Laughter for Health.com, Therapeutic Humor--Laughter for Health and Happiness." Available at http://www.laughterforhealth.com/index.html (accessed July 6, 2010.)

Balch, Phyllis A. Prescription for Herbal Healing. New York: Avery, 2002.

________, and James F. Balch. Prescription for Nutritional Healing. New York: Avery, 2000.

Bowden, Jonny. The 150 Healthiest Foods on Earth. Gloucester: Fair Winds Press, 2007.

Clevely, Andi; Katherine Richmond; Sallie Morris; and Lesley Mackley. Cooking with Herbs and Spice. London: Hermes House, 2003.

Eker, T. Harv. Secrets of the Millionaire Mind: Mastering the Inner Game of Wealth. New York City: Harper Business, 2005.

Hicks, Ester and Jerry. The Law of Attraction: the Basics of the Teachings of Abraham. Carlesbad: Hay House, Inc., 2006.

Herring, Jeff. "Goal Setting & Goal Getting: Consistent-Persistent-Resistant," Ezine Articles. Available at http://ezinearticles.com/?Goal-Setting-and-Goal-Getting:-Consistent---Persistent--Resistant&id=109061 (accessed July 2010.)

Jaret, Peter, "A Healthy Mix of Rest and Motion." New York Times, May 3, 2007,http://www.nytimes.com/2007/05/03/fashion/03Fitness.html?r=1 (accessed July 5, 2010.)

Mateljan, George. "The World's Healthiest Foods." The George Mateljan Foundation. Availalbe at http://www.whfoods.org/foodstoc.php.

Mercola, Joseph. "Take Control of Your Health." Available at http://www.articles.mercola.com/sites/current.aspx.

Newton BBS Home Page. 22 March, 2004. Vanhoeck. Ask a Scientist, Molecular Biology Archive. 25 March, 2009. Available at http://www.newton.dep.anl.gov/askasci/mole00/mole00482.htm.

Roizen, Michael F., and John La Puma. The RealAge Diet. New York: HarperCollins, 2001.

Swindoll, Chuck R. "Insight for Living." Available at http://www.insight.org/about/chuck-swindoll.html.

Talanain, Jason L., et al., "Two weeks of high-intensity aerobic interval training increases the capacity for fat oxidation during exercise in women." *Journal of Applied Physiology 102:1439-1447 (2006). Available at http://jap.physiology.org/cgi/content/abstract/102/4/1439 (accessed July 5, 2010.)*

Tolle, Eckhart. A New Earth: Awakening to Your Life's Purpose. London: Plume, 2006.

________. The Power of Now: A Guide to Spiritual Enlightenment. Novato: New World Library, 1999.

About the Author

My name is Christia Sale, and I'm just like you.

I've reached midlife, and I have children who are sprouting their wings. But what brings me here today is that I have survived a rough marriage, and an even rougher divorce. And it was ***HELL!*** And I'm here to tell you that you don't have to be miserable anymore!

I was raised in an environment where family was *the* most important thing. So it was sad when I realized, at the beginning of my marriage, mind you, that I had made a big mistake. But by then I was already pregnant. I was also raised to believe that I should do everything possible to make the marriage work when there were children involved. So, I thought that if I tried hard enough, he would come around and realize how lucky he was to have a loving family. But he wasn't used to that dynamic. Can you say dysfunctional childhood? I thought that I could "love" him to health. What was *I* thinking? I didn't know any better. I'm a hopeless romantic.

I got so caught up in trying to make my marriage work that I totally lost myself in the process. Then I finally realized that nothing was going to save the relationship that I spent 17 years giving CPR to.

I woke up one morning and had an epiphany. "***Screw this!*** Life is too short to be so unhappy. I don't *deserve* to be treated this way. No one does! I am ***SO*** out of here!"

And that was all I needed. I was done. I was finished putting an egocentric, passive-aggressive (stop me now before I really get started!) husband's needs above my own, and I was tired of living in a one-sided relationship. The thought of staying in that situation for the rest of my life made my skin ***crawl.*** My time here was ***over!*** I deserved better! **It was my turn, Dammit!**

You know, for years of always being last on the needs list, thinking that was what "good mother's" do, I can't truly convey how liberating it was to put a stop to the madness. Yes, I don't mind caring for my children and parents because I love them dearly, but if I can't get my basic emotional needs met from my supposed spouse, and I'm talking years of it, ***I'm done!*** To Hell with that! I mean really, life is too short to live that way with nothing but heartache in return. Can you imagine when the kids were gone and it was just going to be me and *him* - not just ***NO*** but ***HELL NO!*** The thought of that gives me chills!

Even with my adamant decision for *freedom*, it still took about two years of healing to get my mojo back. I had to let myself mourn the loss of the "dream" . . . the dream of a happy marriage. It took a lot of praying, affirmations, exercising, sleeping, and healthy eating to bring me back to the land of the living. *Can I get an Amen!*

There are still a few issues I need to deal with though. One is accepting the fact that I'm never going to reach my svelte weight again. You know, when I could still see my hip bones? It would take more energy and obsessive focus than I'm willing to give it. At my age, it would be a full time job, *and* it would just make me *grumpy!* Second, those little wrinkles . . . I have to accept the fact that *life* has been creeping across my face when I wasn't looking. What's up with that? Do you think Dr. Perricone makes house calls? And last, but not least, I have to delete those annoying little tapes that I keep hearing in the shadows of my mind that say "You're not good enough to make it work."

After a "challenging" marriage, shall we say, I was completely depleted of my energy, and my power. I couldn't even recognize myself in the mirror anymore. In the final stages of trying to resuscitate that lost cause, I aged 10 years in a 3-year period. Life had taken its toll on my face, and body. I needed to get back in touch with my true spirit and zest for life. I needed to find my "self" again. The only way I knew how to accomplish this was "out with the old and in with the new."

During that unhappy period of my life, I internalized my stress and sadness, giving me irritable bowel syndrome. I drank too much, drying out my skin. I cried a lot and didn't sleep much, ruining my face. Not a good combination for that "youthful glow!" Can you say wrinkles? My soul was sad and empty.

But after letting myself mourn the loss of the *"dream"* of a happy marriage, I eventually started getting my zest back. I searched my soul for what I really wanted from life. Because if not now, when? I fed my body with healthy, natural foods that nurtured my cells and my soul. I started exercising with a purpose. I lost that "lifeless" look in my skin. I started losing that swollen look in my body. And my stomach stopped hurting all the time. I started looking and feeling like my old self again. *Can I get another Amen!*

Life is *too* short not to be happy. This life was given to us to enjoy, not to be miserable. It was also given to us to make this world a better place than it was when we got here. You can't accomplish any of this if you don't feel dynamic, vibrant, balanced, and happy. And face it, when we regain control of our outlook *and* outcome, we are much more likely to have a positive impact on the rest of our world.

Having reached midlife, I have realized that I *still* have another half of my life to be the best I can be. And being healthy and happy are key components to making that happen. And it is easier to maintain than you think. No matter what your circumstances, if you are nurturing your body, spirit and soul, eating clean and lean, staying active mentally and physically, and being true to your goals, you will have the balance needed to be a beacon of light in this world. Shine on Sister!

As most wives and mothers can relate to, my needs were always on the back burner. But knowing that I'm finally paying attention to **myself first** is very empowering. My attitude is much more dynamic, my disposition is much happier, and my response to life is much more balanced.

Doing the things I want to do, when I want to do them is all about ***ME***. Taking time to exercise is something I do just for me. Eating clean, lean foods makes me feel more vibrant. Affirmations make me feel more appreciative. Setting goals for my life and accomplishing them makes me more in control. These things I do for ***ME***!

Because It's My Turn! Dammit!